ROBERT L. MILLET AND LLOYD D. NEWELL

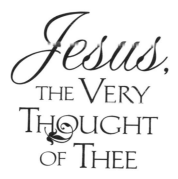

Jesus,
THE VERY
THOUGHT
OF THEE

DAILY REFLECTIONS ON
THE NEW TESTAMENT

EAGLE
GATE

SALT LAKE CITY, UTAH

Visit us at www.deseretbook.com

Library of Congress Cataloging-in-Publication Data

Millet, Robert L.
    Jesus, the very thought of thee : daily reflections on the New Testament / Robert L. Millet, Lloyd D. Newell.
        p.   cm.
    Includes bibliographical references and index.
    ISBN 1-57008-860-8 (alk. paper)
    1. Bible. N.T.—Devotional literature.   2. Devotional calendars—Church of Jesus Christ of Latter-day Saints. 3. Church of Jesus Christ of Latter-day Saints—Prayer-books and devotions—English.   I. Newell, Lloyd D., 1956-   II. Title.
    BS2341.55 .M55 2002
    242'.2—dc21   2002010643

Printed in the United States of America   42316-300214
Inland Press, Menomonee Falls, WI

10   9   8   7   6   5   4

To our wives
Karmel Newell and Shauna Millet
whose quiet and constant Christian examples
point us to the abundant life

PREFACE

Prophets ancient and modern have encouraged the Saints to search the scriptures and to strive to find new insights and new applications with each reading. In his great Intercessory Prayer, the Savior pleaded with the Father, "Sanctify [the disciples] through thy truth: thy word is truth" (John 17:17). That same Lord has called upon the Latter-day Saints to "treasure up in your minds continually the words of life" (D&C 84:85).

We become what we think about. It is incumbent upon those who claim to be disciples of Christ to reflect frequently and consistently upon holy writ, to ponder intently upon the word of the Lord and the teachings of his prophets.

Jesus, the Very Thought of Thee is a kind of guided tour through the New Testament, from Matthew through Revelation, with daily reflections upon New Testament passages. But it is not just a book of inspirational sayings. Rather, each day we ponder a doctrinal principle or precept that flows from the teachings of Jesus and his apostles and draw upon latter-day scripture and modern prophets for clarification and insight. Many times we suggest the personal relevance of a given passage; other times we simply present the teachings and leave you to discover new meaning for yourself.

Like you, we long for the same experience the risen Lord had with the two disciples on the road to Emmaus. Jesus "expounded unto them in all the scriptures the things concerning himself." After Christ had left them, "they said one to another, Did not our heart burn within us, while he talked with us by the way, and while he opened to us the scriptures?" (Luke 24:27, 32.) The scriptures contain the word of God, and there is power in his word. That you may be edified and fortified in your faith through the pages of this book is our sincere prayer.

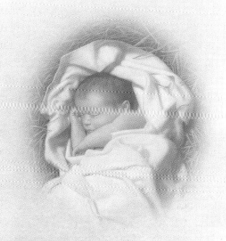

JANUARY

For unto you is born this day in
the city of David a Saviour, which
is Christ the Lord. And this shall
be a sign unto you; Ye shall find a
babe wrapped in swaddling clothes,
lying in a manger.

—LUKE 2:11-12

JANUARY 1

The beginning of the gospel of Jesus Christ, the Son of God.
—MARK 1:1

None of us is bright enough or powerful enough to save ourselves or to face life and its challenges alone. We must have help. Were it not for divine assistance, each of us would falter and fail and lose the battle of life. "Thanks be to God, which giveth us the victory through our Lord Jesus Christ" (1 Corinthians 15:57). The message of peace, the proclamation of hope from the beginning, is that there is a means of recovery, a system of salvation by which fallen men and women can be redeemed and restored to peace and happiness and glory. That system is the gospel of Jesus Christ, the good news or glad tidings that "he came into the world, even Jesus, to be crucified for the world, and to bear the sins of the world, and to sanctify the world, and to cleanse it from all unrighteousness" (D&C 76:41).

In the beginning was the gospel preached through the Son. And
the gospel was the word, and the word was with the Son,
and the Son was with God, and the Son was of God.
—JST JOHN 1:1

From modern revelation we know that the gospel of Jesus Christ has been taught from the beginning of time on earth (Moses 5:1–8; 6:51–62). Indeed, this everlasting system of salvation, the plan of the Eternal Father, was taught by God our Father in the councils of heaven before we were born into mortality. In that "first estate" (Jude 1:6; Abraham 3:26), Jehovah—one "like unto God" (Abraham 3:24), the greatest of all the spirit children of the Father—became the chief advocate and proponent of the Father's plan. He thereby became the "Lamb slain from the foundation of the world" (Revelation 13:8; Moses 7:47). In an act of consummate consecration, the Master set the pattern for his earthly ministry with these words: "Father, thy will be done, and the glory be thine forever" (Moses 4:2).

*That was the true Light, which lighteth every man
that cometh into the world.*

—JOHN 1:9

Everyone born into the world is given the light of Christ so that each "may know good from evil" (Moroni 7:16). This light chases darkness away and illuminates the path back to God (D&C 50:25; 84:46). The world entices us with counterfeit lights, but following those lights makes it difficult to find the true Light again. A loving Father in Heaven, who does not want us to stumble in the darkness, gave us the Light of the World to kindle our souls. Like a tiny ray of sunshine in a dark cave, the light of Christ grows brighter as we draw nearer to it. It blesses us with discernment and activates our agency so that we can see the difference between right and wrong, the important and the less important. Repentance, faithfulness, and obedience help us feel its warmth as it grows "brighter and brighter until the perfect day" (D&C 50:24).

He came unto his own, and his own received him not.
But as many as received him, to them gave he power to become
the sons of God, even to them that believe on his name.
—JOHN 1:11–12

Some who walked and talked with Christ failed to find their salvation in him, yet others, even before he was born, received him as their Redeemer. Those who follow Jesus by faith and righteousness are endowed with power to become the sons and daughters of Christ by adoption into his family. Through the covenant of baptism and a lifetime of hearts being changed through faith on his name, we are given power through the Atonement to become his children (Revelation 21:7; Mosiah 5:7; D&C 39:4). We receive the first principles and ordinances of the gospel, enter into the sacred ordinances and covenants of the temple, and faithfully walk the gospel path. Imbued with the Spirit, we become joint-heirs with Christ and receive with him a glorious exaltation in the kingdom of the Father (Romans 8:14–18; D&C 76:54–60; 84:33–41).

And no man hath seen God at any time,
except he hath borne record of the Son;
for except it is through him no man can be saved.
—JST JOHN 1:19

Foundational to our faith in the restored gospel of Jesus Christ is Joseph Smith's First Vision. That grand theophany ushered in the dawning of a new day, a restoration of truth, a new dispensation of light and knowledge. Following the pattern of priesthood government set forth in the scriptures, God the Eternal Father appeared in a grove of trees made sacred by the experience. He declared to the young prophet, *"This is My Beloved Son. Hear Him!"* (Joseph Smith–History 1:17). All revelation from God to man since the fall of Adam has been by and through Jehovah, who is Jesus Christ. Whenever the Father has appeared on this earth, as he did in 1820, it has been to introduce and bear record of the Son (Smith, *Doctrines of Salvation,* 1:27).

The angel said unto her, Fear not, Mary:
for thou hast found favour with God.
And, behold, thou shalt conceive in thy womb,
and bring forth a son, and shalt call his name JESUS.
—LUKE 1:30–31

The angel's salutation, "Fear not," resounds in the hearts of all who have faith in Jesus Christ. "Perfect love casteth out fear" (1 John 4:18), and he is the embodiment of that perfect love. Named in the heavens and in prophetic utterance through the ages, he is the promised Messiah, the Only Begotten of the Father, the Lord God Omnipotent who made flesh his tabernacle (Mosiah 3:5). He is the One by whom salvation comes, the only perfect person who has ever walked the earth, who suffered inconceivable pain and anguish, who gave his life that we might be spiritually begotten as his sons and daughters (Acts 4:12; 2 Nephi 25:20). The Son of an immortal Personage, Jesus was born to a beautiful virgin mother in a lowly stable. He came to redeem us, to show us the way, to fulfill all righteousness, and to assuage our fears. He came that we might live—and live abundantly.

*And Mary said, Behold the handmaid of the Lord;
be it unto me according to thy word.*
—LUKE 1:38

With perfect humility, the chosen virgin submitted to the will of God. The magnificent heavenly announcement was still incomprehensible to her—so young and so pure. Yet, faithful and meek, she obeyed. "This affirmation of submission, conformity, and obedience—yes, even of anxious willingness to do the will of Deity—ranks in sublimity and majesty with the declaration of the pre-existent Christ, who responding to the Father's search for a Redeemer, volunteered: 'Father, thy will be done, and the glory be thine forever' (Moses 4:2)" (McConkie, *Doctrinal New Testament Commentary,* 1:84). We, too, can humbly surrender our all on the heavenly altar. We may not grasp the full meaning; we may feel overwhelmed with what lies ahead. But we can trust God's goodness, know of his perfect love, and find comfort that he knows all things and desires for us unspeakable happiness. Humbly and joyfully, we can respond, "Thy will be done."

When as his mother Mary was espoused to Joseph,
before they came together,
she was found with child of the Holy Ghost.
—MATTHEW 1:18

We rejoice in the truth restored in our day that God is an exalted man, a "Man of Holiness" (Moses 6:57), and we are his spirit sons and daughters. The ancient prophets foretold that Mary, "a virgin, a precious and chosen vessel," would be "overshadowed and conceive by the power of the Holy Ghost, and bring forth a son, yea, even the Son of God" (Alma 7:10). Jesus of Nazareth was man, but more than man; he was teacher, but more than teacher. The power of his person and of his message lay in who he was. President Ezra Taft Benson taught: "The Church of Jesus Christ of Latter-day Saints proclaims that Jesus Christ is the Son of God in the most literal sense. The body in which He performed His mission in the flesh was sired by that same Holy Being we worship as God, our Eternal Father" (*Come unto Christ,* 4).

And she brought forth her firstborn son,
and wrapped him in swaddling clothes, and laid him in a manger;
because there was no room for them in the inn.
—Luke 2:7

Mary and Joseph had gone home to Bethlehem, to Joseph's "own city" (Luke 2:3), but no one received them. Then, as now, the real problem was not one of space. Room might have been found in the inn for someone else but not for Joseph and Mary. Instead, they welcomed the newborn King of kings to a cave-stable in the company of animals. As an adult, Jesus would say, "I came unto mine own, and mine own received me not" (D&C 10:57; 45:8). But no matter what he did not receive, he still freely gives. He rescues those for whom accommodations are otherwise refused. He welcomes the outsider. He brings the light of life to the darkest caverns and the coldest hearts. And to those of his own household, he returned "beauty for ashes, the oil of joy for mourning, the garment of praise for the spirit of heaviness" (Isaiah 61:3).

The angel said unto them, Fear not: for, behold,
I bring you good tidings of great joy, which shall be to all people.
For unto you is born this day in the city of David a Saviour,
which is Christ the Lord.

—LUKE 2:10–11

The angel's declaration to the shepherds, "Fear not," was a theme of the Lord's life that began before he was born (Luke 1:30) and continued through his life (Matthew 1:20; 14:27; John 14:27) and even after his resurrection (Matthew 28:10). Jesus would save us from fear, if only we put our faith in him. But after two thousand years, do we still fear the cost of following Christ? His message cannot comfort us if we allow his peace to be overshadowed by our anxiety and fear. His forgiveness cannot take effect until we open our hearts to his love. The babe of Bethlehem came not just to the house of Israel, not just to a favored few in a distant land. His saving message is for everyone (D&C 133:37). When we "fear not" and trust in him, we find safety, direction, and peace. We are filled with love and feel the great joy of the good tidings of Christ.

But Mary kept all these things, and pondered them in her heart.
—LUKE 2:19

Luke tells us much about the faith of a mother—and the process of revelation. Righteous parents seek for divine direction as they rear God's children. Though they know a child's earthly beginnings, they don't know how the child's life will unfold. As time goes on, parents recognize their child's unique gifts and capabilities, real potential—and also areas of concern. They seek divine guidance. The Lord instructed Oliver Cowdery on the spirit of revelation: "I will tell you in your mind and in your heart, by the Holy Ghost, which shall come upon you and which shall dwell in your heart. Now, behold, this is the spirit of revelation" (D&C 8:2–3). As parents prayerfully ponder, their thoughts (mind) and their feelings (heart) come together, and they can receive divine direction, usually one step at a time. Like Mary, they trust God, pondering his word and seeking more direction at each step along the way.

The book of the generation of Jesus Christ,
the son of David, the son of Abraham.
—MATTHEW 1:1

Very early in the Gospels of Matthew and Luke we encounter the genealogy of Jesus and such obscure names as Phares and Esrom and Ozias and Salathiel and Eliud. What difference do those names make to you or me? Perhaps it is important for us as followers of the Master to know that while our Lord was indeed the Son of Man, he was also the son of man, a human being. He didn't suddenly drop out of heaven; he was born at a certain place in a certain time of earth's history, just as we are. He had ancestors, men and women who were mortal, frail, and in need of divine mercy and grace, just as we are. Jesus is therefore "touched with the feeling of our infirmities" (Hebrews 4:15). He knows "the weakness of man and how to succor them who are tempted" (D&C 62:1). He knows. He understands.

And when they had opened their treasures,
they presented unto him gifts; gold,
and frankincense, and myrrh.
—MATTHEW 2:11

The coming of the Lord of Life signaled what we call the meridian of time, the high point in the history of the salvation of humankind. Such a vital moment did not take place without announcement to those who were attuned to the Spirit. About two years after the birth of Jesus (Matthew 2:16), wise men from the East, seeking the "Messiah of the Jews" (JST Matthew 3:2), were led to the home of Mary and Joseph. These wise men, sensitive souls who were perhaps Jews of the dispersion, worshiped their Messiah and gave him precious gifts in celebration of the coming of the Promised One. Their gifts had both monetary value and symbolic meaning. Christians through the generations have acknowledged gold as a symbol of Jesus' royalty, frankincense as a sign of his divinity, and myrrh as a poignant foreshadowing of his death and burial.

*Then Herod . . . slew all the children that were in Bethlehem,
and in all the coasts thereof, from two years old and under.*
—MATTHEW 2:16

New Testament scholars estimate that, given the population of Bethlehem at the time (about a thousand), the "slaughter of the innocents" probably involved the deaths of about twenty male children. This senseless act, like the decree pronounced anciently by Pharaoh before the birth of Moses (Exodus 1:8–22), dramatizes the paranoid and wicked frenzy that characterized the mind and heart of the ruler ironically designated by history as Herod the Great. This heinous act is but another illustration of Satan's fruitless efforts to thwart the accomplishment of the purposes of God. The Saints of the Most High move forward, despite such opposition, trusting the prophetic promise that "no weapon that is formed against thee shall prosper" (Isaiah 54:17; D&C 71:9).

After three days they found him in the temple. . . . And all who
heard him were astonished at his understanding. . . . And his
mother said unto him, Son, why hast thou thus dealt with
us? . . . And he said unto them, . . . Knew ye not
that I must be about my Father's business?
—JST LUKE 2:46–49

Under Jewish law, at age twelve Jesus became a son of the law and subject to its obligations: participate in the annual Passover celebration, enter the temple courts, ask and answer questions, and listen to the learned rabbis. That he was in the temple at age twelve is not unusual, but the knowledge and understanding he demonstrated there were astonishing. Jesus knew that he was the Son of God. In response to his mother's inquiry, he offered his first recorded testimony that God was his Father. Neither a criticism nor a reproof, the Son of God simply clarified that he knew what both Mary and Joseph knew. He who was perfect, even at age twelve, offered no disregard for loving earthly parents who had taught and nurtured him for his first twelve years. His gentle word was in fact not just a statement about who he was but also a sobering reminder about the road ahead.

And Jesus increased in wisdom and stature,
and in favour with God and man.
—LUKE 2:52

Jesus' home during the first decades of his mortal life was Nazareth, where he lived a relatively simple life as a carpenter's son. Just as with us, a veil of forgetfulness was drawn across his mind, but as he matured physically, mentally, socially, and spiritually, a full sense of his mission as the Messiah developed within his soul. "He received not of the fulness at first, but continued from grace to grace, until he received a fulness" (D&C 93:13). His learning came not through error but through experience and revelation. He advanced from one grace to another, from good to greater good, from favor with God to greater favor. We too grow line upon line, precept upon precept, learning a bit today, improving tomorrow, and, hopefully, progressing spiritually before we pass through the veil of death. Like him, we develop our relationships with others as we refine our relationship with God.

And he served under his father,
and he spake not as other men, neither could he be taught;
for he needed not that any man should teach him.
And after many years, the hour of his ministry drew nigh.
—JST MATTHEW 3:25–26

There can be no doubt that Mary and Joseph were chosen for their sacred assignment before the foundations of this earth were laid. Nothing was left to chance when it came to the birth, home life, and training of the child who was to grow up and become the Savior and Redeemer of all humankind. It was needful that Jesus be brought up "in the nurture and admonition of the Lord" (Ephesians 6:4; Enos 1:1), that he be loved and valued and taught in such a way as to point him toward righteousness and truth. But there were with Jesus, as there are with each of us, some things that no mortal man or woman could teach (1 John 2:27). Some lessons can only be learned as the veil becomes thin and eternal truth distills upon sensitive souls as the dews from heaven.

Think not to say within yourselves,
We have Abraham to our father: for I say unto you,
that God is able of these stones to raise up
children unto Abraham.
—MATTHEW 3:9

Jesus, the Lion of the tribe of Judah (Revelation 5:5), boldly declared to the Jews of his day that the only true aristocracy in the kingdom of God is the aristocracy of righteousness. Descendants of Abraham are not saved because Abraham once passed severe tests of faith, nor are descendants of Joseph exalted in the highest heaven because Joseph of old stood firm in defense of truth and virtue. Although a person's heritage may provide an example by which to live and a moral reinforcement during trying times, only those who choose to come unto Christ by covenant are his chosen people. As Paul explained, among the household of faith, "ye are all one in Christ Jesus. And if ye be Christ's, then are ye Abraham's seed, and heirs according to the promise" (Galatians 3:28–29; 2 Nephi 30:2).

*And the people asked [John the Baptist], saying, What shall we
do then? He answereth and saith unto them,
He that hath two coats, let him impart to him that hath none;
and he that hath meat, let him do likewise.*
—LUKE 3:10—11

The call to Christian discipleship is a call, first of all,
to come unto Christ and be changed, to have our sins
remitted through baptism and our guilt washed away.
Thereafter, as John the Baptist affirms, it is a call to
change our lives, to live what we espouse, to mourn
with those who mourn and bear the burdens of those
whose hearts are heavy (Mosiah 18:8—9). It is a call to
inconvenience, an invitation to take up the cross daily,
to give and forgive, to reach out and welcome back. To
come unto Christ is to begin to acquire the attributes
of Christ and thereby embody pure religion (James
1:27).

Then cometh Jesus . . . unto John, to be baptized of him. But John forbad him, saying, I have need to be baptized of thee, and comest thou to me? And Jesus answering said unto him, Suffer it to be so now: for thus it becometh us to fulfil all righteousness.
—MATTHEW 3:13–15

Because Jesus was without sin, he was not baptized for the remission of sins. Rather, he was baptized to fulfill all righteousness. He was the only sinless person ever to walk the earth, the only one whose every word, thought, and deed were always in accord with his Father's will. With perfect humility, he covenanted with his Father that he would willingly keep all of his commandments. He showed us that there are indispensable ordinances requisite for salvation in the kingdom of God. He marked the path and showed the way that we must follow (2 Nephi 31:4–12).

Then Jesus was led up of the Spirit,
into the wilderness, to be with God.
—JST MATTHEW 4:1

The Joseph Smith Translation clarifies the New
Testament statement that Jesus went into the wilderness "to be tempted of the devil" (Matthew 4:1). The
father of all lies needs no help to do his work, but all
of us, even the Son of God, need preparation to do the
work of the Father. Moses encountered Deity on the
holy mountain and was taught the purposes of God to
prepare him for his monumental task of leading Israel
out of Egyptian bondage. After his dramatic conversion, Saul of Tarsus spent three years in Arabia and
Damascus before meeting with Church leaders at
Jerusalem, a period which no doubt entailed much
soul searching and reorientation. In that same spirit,
Jesus sought to commune with the Father in preparation for his singular ministry. As his brother later
wrote: "Resist the devil, and he will flee from you.
Draw nigh to God, and he will draw nigh to you"
(James 4:7–8).

And when the devil had ended all the temptation,
he departed from him for a season.
—LUKE 4:13

Luke is the only Gospel writer to record that the devil left the Master "for a season," yet afterward, surely Satan dogged Jesus' steps throughout his ministry, seeking with a vengeance to ensnare him whose actions and feelings needed always to remain pure. Those assaults were magnified in unimaginable ways during the hours of alienation in Gethsemane. But Jesus did not yield. Thus, although Christ was "in all points tempted like as we are, yet [he remained] without sin" (Hebrews 4:15; 1 Peter 2:21–22). Joseph Smith explained that Jesus "kept the law of God, and remained without sin, showing thereby that it is in the power of man to keep the law and remain also without sin; and also, that by him a righteous judgment might come upon all flesh, and that all who walk not in the law of God may justly be condemned by the law, and have no excuse" (*Lectures on Faith* 5:2).

Master, . . . where dwellest thou?
He saith unto them, Come and see.
—JOHN 1:38–39

"Come and see" is an invitation and a promise to all of God's children. "Come and see" is opening our hearts to his redeeming love and casting our burdens at his feet (Matthew 11:28–29). "Come and see" is giving away all our sins that we might know him (Alma 22:18). "Come and see" is discovering who he truly is and who we really are. "Come and see" is becoming a devoted member of his Church, experiencing lasting joy and "peace in this world, and eternal life in the world to come" (D&C 59:23). As Elder Alexander B. Morrison invites, "Come to Him . . . ; recognize in Him the great Messiah who will come again with healing in His wings, to set His people free. He will wrap you about in the cloak of His redeeming love, and your life will be changed forever" (*Ensign,* November 2000, 13).

*One of the two which heard John [the Baptist] speak,
and followed him, was Andrew, Simon Peter's brother. He first
findeth his own brother Simon, and saith unto him, We have
found the Messias, which is, being interpreted, the Christ.*
—JOHN 1:40–41

The hearts of Andrew and Peter were "brim with joy" because they had found the Messiah, the Anointed One (Alma 26:11). The Hope of Israel, the promised Savior, had come. The condescension of the Lord God Omnipotent, the God of Abraham, Isaac, and Jacob, was underway. Like these ancient Galileans, men and women of all walks of life seek for peace— and peace is found only in Christ. They seek for fulfillment and purpose—and these are found only in Christ. They yearn for meaningful answers to life's hard questions, answers that come only in and through Him who is the Way, the Truth, and the Life. The quest for the Jesus of history is far less vital than the search for the Christ of faith. The promise to men and women everywhere is "Draw near unto me and I will draw near unto you; seek me diligently and ye shall find me" (D&C 88:63).

*Philip findeth Nathanael, and saith unto him, We have found
him, of whom Moses in the law, and the prophets, did write, Jesus
of Nazareth, the son of Joseph. And Nathanael said unto him,
Can there any good thing come out of Nazareth?
Philip saith unto him, Come and see.*

—JOHN 1:45–46

From Nazareth, an obscure village in Galilee, did
Jesus come to save all people. That he would come
from such a place tells us something about him and his
Father—and about ourselves. Nathanael's question
echoes down the centuries: Do we miss the message
of salvation because it comes simply, without fanfare
and ostentation? Do we pass over the meek Nazarene
because we're looking for something more spectacu-
lar? In our own relationships, do we disparage those
who come from humble backgrounds, from the wrong
side of the tracks? Do we sometimes disregard those
who seem of little importance or modest means? The
Savior's life teaches us otherwise. He would have us
look past labels and get to know the real person.
"Come and see." Come drink deeply from the well of
living water (John 4:13–14). See how the Nazarene
can change our hearts and bring us peace and salvation.

*Jesus answered and said unto him [Nicodemus], Verily, verily,
I say unto thee, Except a man be born again,
he cannot see the kingdom of God.*
—JOHN 3:3

Because they are Gods, our Heavenly Father and his
Son Jesus Christ are forevermore involved in change.
Placing Adam and Eve and all forms of life on the
earth at the Creation changed things. The Fall precipi-
tated dramatic change. Then Jesus came to earth to
change men and women—to reverse a downward
trend that would otherwise continue toward dissolution. The gospel of Jesus Christ is all about change.
Betterment. Improvement. Refinement. Transformation. To choose Christ is to choose to be changed, to
be born again, to come alive to things of righteousness,
to become a new creation of the Holy Ghost. Without
such a change, we cannot see the kingdom of God,
cannot recognize revealed truth and the relevance of
that truth to our own lives. Through such a rebirth or
conversion, we become attentive to a higher way of
life, sensitive to spiritual things, enticed by goodness,
attracted to holiness.

*The wind bloweth where it listeth, and thou hearest the sound
thereof, but canst not tell whence it cometh, and whither it goeth:
so is every one that is born of the Spirit.*
—JOHN 3:8

I magine a father saying to his twelve-year-old son,
"If you have any respect for me as your father, you will
grow to be six foot eight." Such a request would be
cruel and unkind, because the son has little control
over how tall he will become. He can eat the right
foods, train and work out, and do everything in his
power to grow big and strong, but some things he cannot control. Similarly, spiritual experience is not completely under our control. We cannot prepare plans
that will always result in predictable spiritual phenomena. We can provide a setting for growth, but we
must then exercise patience and trust in the Lord and
his purposes. We cannot force spiritual things. God
will bring miracles into our lives if we are true and
faithful, but they will come "in his own time, and in
his own way, and according to his own will" (D&C
88:68).

And as Moses lifted up the serpent in the wilderness,
even so must the Son of man be lifted up: That whosoever
believeth in him should not perish, but have eternal life.
—JOHN 3:14–15

Truly, "all things are created and made to bear record of [Christ], both things which are temporal, and things which are spiritual" (Moses 6:63). From the beginning, prophets have urged men and women to look forward with an eye of faith to the eternal atoning sacrifice of Jesus Christ. Just as the ancient Israelites who had been bitten by the fiery flying serpents were healed when they looked to the brazen serpent held high by Moses, so are we spared the pain of sin and death when we "look to God and live" (Alma 37:47). Just as Christ was lifted up into immortality by the Father, so are we lifted up as we look to the Lord— lifted above our fears, lifted above our weakness, lifted above our limitations. The Captain of our salvation (Hebrews 2:10) beckons unto us, "Look unto me in every thought; doubt not, fear not" (D&C 6:36).

For God so loved the world, that he gave his only begotten Son,
that whosoever believeth in him should not perish,
but have everlasting life.
—JOHN 3:16

Twenty-five words uttered by Jesus (JST John 3:18) summarize the entire gospel plan, tying together the Father, the Son, and his atoning sacrifice and affirming God's encompassing love for his children. Salvation comes only through Christ: "There shall be no other name given nor any other way nor means whereby salvation can come unto the children of men, only in and through the name of Christ, the Lord Omnipotent" (Mosiah 3:17). The Savior "so loved the world that he gave his own life, that as many as would believe might become the sons of God" (D&C 34:3). As we live his teachings and receive his image in our countenances, we experience a mighty change of heart (Alma 5:14). Then, even though we die, we do not perish. The Savior makes it possible for the faithful to have everlasting life, to receive exaltation in his kingdom with his Father.

Every one that doeth evil hateth the light, neither cometh to the light, lest his deeds should be reproved. But he that doeth truth cometh to the light, that his deeds may be made manifest, that they are wrought in God.

—JOHN 3:20–21

Truth is light. When we embrace truth, we embrace light. "That which is of God is light; and he that receiveth light, and continueth in God, receiveth more light; and that light groweth brighter and brighter until the perfect day. . . . I say it that you may know the truth, that you may chase darkness from among you" (D&C 50:24–25). As we humbly and actively align our lives with his truth, we receive more light. Truth is found in living the type of life exemplified by the Savior, who is "the way, the truth, and the life" (John 14:6). Living truthfully means knowing truth and having the courage to act upon it. Faithfully walking in truth brings us more of the light of truth, deepens our resolve to follow and become more like Jesus, and makes unshakeable our commitment to the gospel. Living the truth becomes a way of life, a key to life eternal.

He [Jesus] must increase, but I [John the Baptist] must decrease.
—JOHN 3:30

Once the Savior of all mankind began his public ministry, it was time for the Elias of preparation, the forerunner, to move into the shadows so that all eyes might be focused on the Light of the World. There is singular majesty in the humble statement of John the Baptist. He recognized that each one of us is a reflection of Christ, who is the Light (3 Nephi 18:24). Our task, our sacred assignment, is to teach his gospel and point others to the Way, the Truth, the Life—the Light (John 14:6; 3 Nephi 11:11).

FEBRUARY

*And Jesus increased in
wisdom and stature, and in
favour with God and man.*

—LUKE 2:52

*Jesus answered and said unto her, If thou knewest the gift of God,
and who it is that saith to thee, Give me to drink; thou wouldest
have asked of him, and he would have given thee living water.*

—JOHN 4:10

Many in our day are dying of thirst while the cooling waters of life are within reach. Some are unaware deliverance is available. Others, tragically, are not even conscious they thirst. "My people have committed two evils," Jehovah said through Jeremiah. "They have forsaken me the fountain of living waters, and hewed them out cisterns, broken cisterns, that can hold no water" (Jeremiah 2:13). In their quest for the living water, many choose alternate paths, irresponsible, unproductive, and empty strategies. We can feel and become all that we were intended to, but it will come about in the Lord's own way, through laboring in his cause, reaching out to others, and seeking through his atonement to be changed and renewed. Chasing worldly fads does not satisfy. Climbing society's ladders does not fulfill. Peace comes from Christ. On him we must rely. In him only can we rest.

Whosoever drinketh of the water that I shall give him shall never thirst; but the water that I shall give him shall be in him a well of water springing up into everlasting life.
—JOHN 4:14

Without water, we cannot live for long. Without the living water, the words of eternal life, the love of God (1 Nephi 11:25), we ultimately cannot live at all. His water truly satisfies the soul's thirst for righteousness and truth. His water gives life—endless life—to the weak and the weary, to those who despair and feel like giving up. His water is a wellspring, bubbling forth with sustaining blessings that lead to everlasting life (D&C 63:23). Christ is the essential, vital, invigorating Source of life and light. How fitting that we call him and his immortal truth the living water, the only water that completely satisfies, the only water that leads to the greatest gift of God—eternal life (D&C 14:7).

FEBRUARY 3

God is a Spirit: and they that worship him must worship him in spirit and in truth.
—JOHN 4:24

Seeking to provide an elevated perspective, an exalted orientation to the Samaritan woman, Jesus taught her that our Father in Heaven and, for that matter, all other eternal truths, must not be left to mortal imaginings. A better translation of John 4:24 is "God is spirit: and they that worship him must worship him in spirit and in truth." We come unto God our Father—through study, prayer, song, and worship—in a spiritual way, for, as the apostle Paul taught, the things of God are known and understood only by the power of the Spirit of God (1 Corinthians 2:11–14). We cannot know God through intellectual pursuits alone, relying upon scientific experimentation or philosophical analysis. God stands revealed, or he remains forever unknown.

*Now we believe, not because of thy saying: for we have
heard him ourselves, and know that this is indeed the Christ,
the Saviour of the world.*
—JOHN 4:42

Paul declared that "faith cometh by hearing, and
hearing by the word of God" (Romans 10:17). The
Prophet Joseph Smith taught, "Faith comes by hearing the word of God, through the testimony of the
servants of God; that testimony is always attended by
the Spirit of prophecy and revelation" (*Teachings of the
Prophet Joseph Smith,* 148). Souls are stirred and hearts
are converted as the gospel is preached by the power
of the Holy Ghost (2 Nephi 33:1). The people of
Samaria first heard of the Lord Jesus through the testimony of the Samaritan woman, and they believed.
Their first witness came through believing on the faith
of another. Then they themselves heard the divine
word from the Master Teacher, and as a result they
knew by the Spirit that he was indeed the promised
Messiah (D&C 46:13–14).

And he began to say unto them,
This day is this scripture fulfilled in your ears.
—LUKE 4:21

Jesus' declaration of his identity sounded as blasphemy to the Jews, who knew Isaiah's messianic utterance, "The Spirit of the Lord God is upon me; . . . he hath sent me to bind up the brokenhearted, to proclaim liberty to the captives, and the opening of the prison to them that are bound" (Isaiah 61:1). In essence, Jesus told them he was the promised Messiah, who was, that very day, the fulfillment of Isaiah's prophecy. Jesus knew exactly who he was and what he had come to do. He had been endowed from on high. He was the Atoning One who would succor all who came unto him. He came to break the bands of death and bring deliverance to the dead. His messianic claim would lead to his mortal death but would make possible everlasting life for all humankind. The scriptures are indeed fulfilled in him.

*When Simon Peter saw [the multitude of fishes],
he fell down at Jesus' knees, saying, Depart from me;
for I am a sinful man, O Lord.*
—LUKE 5:8

Latter-day Saints do not subscribe to the doctrine
of human depravity, a position held by most
Christians. At the same time, which of us would not,
like Peter, fall at the feet of the Holy One and confess
our weakness? Who among us would not undergo a
serious moment of introspection as we realized that
before us stood the only perfect person to inhabit this
planet? Indeed, one of the signs of spiritual maturity
is an ever-growing awareness of our total nothingness
without the Lord (Moses 1:10), our utter helplessness
without his atoning power and mercy. Nephi
expressed this feeling, saying, "I am encompassed
about, because of the temptations and the sins which
do so easily beset me. And when I desire to rejoice, my
heart groaneth because of my sins; nevertheless, I
know in whom I have trusted" (2 Nephi 4:18–19).
Our trust, our reliance, our confidence is in the Lord.

*And Jesus went about all Galilee, teaching in their synagogues,
and preaching the gospel of the kingdom, and healing all manner
of sickness and all manner of disease among the people.*
—MATTHEW 4:23

Of all the words that might describe the work of
the Master, he was, first and foremost, a teacher. He
testified. He preached. He imparted gospel truths. He
opened the minds and hearts of men and women to
sacred things and directed their lives toward infinite
and eternal verities. Through his touch and by the
power of his word, many were healed of their physical
afflictions. His teachings—filled with the Spirit of
truth—were themselves a healing balm to aching
hearts. He spoke the pleasing word of God, "the word
which healeth the wounded soul" (Jacob 2:8).

Jesus seeing their faith said unto the sick of the palsy;
Son, be of good cheer; thy sins be forgiven thee.
—MATTHEW 9:2

Offended by Jesus' statements, the scribes—the doctors of the law, the theologians of their day—demanded, "Why doth this man thus speak blasphemies? who can forgive sins but God only?" (Mark 2:7). The Lord replied, "Wherefore is it that ye think evil in your hearts? For is it not easier to say, Thy sins be forgiven thee, than to say, Arise and walk? But I said this that ye may know that the Son of man hath power on earth to forgive sins" (JST Matthew 9:4–6). The same power by which the Lord of life could lay hands on the sick and raise the dead, command the elements, and still the storms is the means by which troubled hearts and sinful souls are reconciled to God and thus renewed. He who cleansed the scab-ridden hands of the leper can purify the heart of one who has strayed from the path of peace.

And as he passed by, he saw Levi the son of Alphaeus sitting at the
receipt of custom, and said unto him, Follow me.
And he arose and followed him.
—MARK 2:14

Better known as Matthew, Levi was a social outcast, a publican, a tax collector, a representative of the hated Romans. As a result of Jesus' call, however, he became one of the Twelve and author of the first Gospel. How could the Savior summon one so despised by his fellow Jews? How could he call into his intimate circle one who served a foreign master? But Christ's call to Matthew tells us much about both of them. Jesus, who knows our hearts and in whom is no imperfection, saw beyond appearances to the inherent goodness and ability in Matthew. In turn, Matthew must have sensed the divine nature of his call, for "he arose and followed [Jesus]" (Mark 2:14). Both disregarded the preconceptions and prejudices of the day; both were despised and hated by many; both united themselves in love and devotion to a cause greater than any human enterprise.

They that are whole have no need of the physician,
but they that are sick: I came not to call the righteous,
but sinners to repentance.
—MARK 2:17

Just as a man does not really desire food until he is hungry," President Ezra Taft Benson taught, "so he does not desire the salvation of Christ until he knows why he needs Christ. No one adequately and properly knows why he needs Christ until he understands and accepts the doctrine of the Fall and its effect upon all mankind" (*A Witness and a Warning*, 33). There is irony in the truth that no one among us is whole, no one who does not require serious attention from the Great Physician. Everyone needs Jesus Christ. Those who insist they can manage on their own may be those most in need of assistance. We cannot fully appreciate the Medicine unless we acknowledge our malady. We cannot rejoice in the Solution until we recognize our problem.

*No man putteth a piece of new cloth unto an old garment,
for . . . the rent is made worse. Neither do men put
new wine into old bottles; else the bottles break.*
—MATTHEW 9:16–17

Just as new cloth should not be sewn onto old, or new wine put into old animal-skin bottles, so should the gospel of Jesus Christ find new place in our hearts. "If any man be in Christ, he is a new creature: old things are passed away; behold, all things are become new" (2 Corinthians 5:17). Jesus commanded us to empty our hearts of old traditions and beliefs and to come unto him with newness of heart—ready to be taught, easy to be entreated. He will fill our souls with the new covenant. The gospel of Jesus Christ is a new commandment, not simply a repair of the old. The Mosaic law was fulfilled by the gospel of Jesus Christ as it was also replaced by the new and everlasting gospel.

*The Son can do nothing of himself, but what he seeth
the Father do: for what things soever he doeth,
these also doeth the Son likewise.*
—JOHN 5:19

Christ had no private agenda, no desire to do things his way, no ambition to chart his own course. He came to earth to do the Father's work. He said, "My meat is to do the will of him that sent me, and to finish his work" (John 4:34). "I can of mine own self do nothing. . . . I seek not mine own will, but the will of the Father which hath sent me" (John 5:30). "I came down from heaven, not to do mine own will, but the will of him that sent me" (John 6:38). "My doctrine is not mine, but his that sent me" (John 7:16). "I and my Father are one" (John 10:30). The greatest joy and contentment in life come to us as we seek to follow the way of the Master—to learn the will of the Father and then to do it.

The Father judgeth no man,
but hath committed all judgment unto the Son.
—JOHN 5:22

Jesus the Christ is our judge, and thanks be to God that he is. We know just how fickle and myopic the judgment of mortal men and women can be. Too often we do not see things as they really are; instead, we see things as *we* are. Jesus, however, having never yielded to sin, is unaffected by the profoundly blinding effect of personal misdeeds. Having never been driven by pride, the Lord can focus on what is best for each of us, "suiting his mercies according to the conditions of the children of men" (D&C 46:15). He is thus "a perfect, just God, and a merciful God also" (Alma 42:15). That merciful Judge stands at the bar of judgment not only to certify us but also to welcome us.

*All that are in the graves shall hear his voice, and shall come forth;
they that have done good, unto the resurrection of life; and they
that have done evil, unto the resurrection of damnation.*
—JOHN 5:28–29

While pondering the fifth chapter of John's Gospel, Joseph Smith and Sidney Rigdon concluded that "if God rewarded every one according to the deeds done in the body, the term 'Heaven,' as intended for the Saints' eternal home, must include more kingdoms than one" (D&C 76, headnote). The Prophet and his scribe in the new translation of the Bible then received what we know as the vision of the glories (D&C 76). This vision, one of the greatest revelations of all time, is a "transcript from the records of the eternal world" (*Teachings of the Prophet Joseph Smith,* 11). It makes known the meaning of the Lord Jesus' words, "In my Father's house are many mansions" (John 14:2). It demonstrates the stern justice and the tender mercy of our Father in Heaven, his eagerness to bless and reward all of his children.

Search the scriptures; for in them ye think ye have eternal life:
and they are they which testify of me.
—JOHN 5:39

It is not uncommon for people, even religious people, to erect sanctuaries to dead prophets while figuratively or even literally stoning living prophets. The living God is forever eager to teach his children through the prophetic word, but we must be receptive to the voice of the living oracle. John's profound statement is not simply an encouragement to read scripture. It is, in fact, a strong invitation to the people of his day—as well as to those today—to open themselves to a new and everlasting covenant, to heed the divine word sent forth to the world through God's Almighty Son. The Savior was saying, in essence, that we think we have eternal life through the old covenant and the past prophets, but we should search the scriptures, for they testify of him.

And he said unto them, The sabbath was made for man,
and not man for the sabbath: Therefore the
Son of man is Lord also of the sabbath.
—MARK 2:27–28

The commandments, laws, and principles of the gospel are given because they lead us to Christ, not as ends in themselves. It is possible to keep the commandments as a checklist that we rigorously itemize, prioritize, and mark off—without also establishing a meaningful relationship with Jesus. The scriptures tell us that laws and principles are given to point the way to Christ (Galatians 3:24; Jacob 4:5; Mosiah 13:30; Alma 13:16; 34:14). We must depend on the living wisdom and grace of the Lawgiver, not merely the law. We know, for example, that Jesus made the Sabbath day. When we sincerely try to remember him, keeping the Sabbath holy is a joy and a blessing. Our faith is strengthened and our hearts are filled with love as we understand that the Sabbath was made for man, and Jesus Christ is Lord of the Sabbath.

He went out into a mountain to pray, and continued all
night in prayer to God. And when it was day,
he called unto him his disciples: and of them he chose twelve,
whom also he named apostles.
—LUKE 6:12–13

*A*postle, the title Jesus gave to those called as special witnesses of his name, means "one sent forth"—one sent forth to bear testimony of the resurrected Christ and boldly proclaim his name throughout the world; one sent forth holding the keys of the priesthood to represent the Savior, to be his agent, and to declare his divinity. Before issuing the call to apostleship, our Lord prayed all night. An apostle himself (Hebrews 3:1–2), as a representative of his Father, he understood what his chosen Twelve would endure in his name. Then and now, twelve men with this same divine commission and ordination constitute the Quorum of the Twelve Apostles. Then and now, these chosen men exercise a divine calling, subordinating all other duties, to stand as witnesses of the name of Christ in all the world (D&C 107:23).

Blessed are the poor in spirit: for theirs is the kingdom of heaven.
—MATTHEW 5:3

To the first of the Beatitudes, the Book of Mormon adds, "Blessed are the poor in spirit *who come unto me*" (3 Nephi 12:3; italics added). There is no salvation in humility alone. Salvation comes to those who humbly approach the Lord to seek reconciliation and transformation. The universal sin of pride is enmity—between humankind and God, and between one person and another. Pride keeps us from the Savior and locks our hearts against everlasting things. If we look down upon others condescendingly or look upwards covetously, we are prideful. Both forms of pride lead to estrangement from God and our fellow beings. Our vainness and foolishness (2 Nephi 9:28) hinder us from growing in covenant relationship with Christ and true intimacy with others. Nothing of worth happens in the spiritual realm—here or hereafter—without humility that leads to Christ.

Blessed are they that mourn: for they shall be comforted.
—MATTHEW 5:4

If we live and love, we will surely mourn; but doom, despair, and discouragement need not be the final chapter of our book of life. Real comfort, the kind of which peace and hope are made, comes from the Lord and from the Holy Ghost, the Comforter. We find comfort in prayer, patient pleading, and humble submission. When trials come, we find comfort in the words of prophets. When troubles hang over us, we seek wisdom from inspired leaders and loved ones. We turn our hearts to the source of everlasting comfort, even the Prince of Peace. When our sorrow seems more than we can bear, we turn to the Lord to find comfort and peace. Because of him, we can give comfort and peace to others. Alma invited all who would covenant with Christ to "mourn with those that mourn; yea, and comfort those that stand in need of comfort" (Mosiah 18:9).

Blessed are the meek: for they shall inherit the earth.
—MATTHEW 5:5

Meekness is not weakness. Jesus does not expect his followers to seek after martyrdom or delight in being persecuted. Meekness is poise under provocation. To be meek is to be in control, to be victorious over self. President Howard W. Hunter explained: "In a world too preoccupied with winning through intimidation and seeking to be number one, no large crowd of folk is standing in line to buy books that call for mere meekness. But the meek shall inherit the earth—a pretty impressive corporate takeover, and done *without* intimidation! Sooner or later—and we pray sooner rather than later—everyone will acknowledge that Christ's way is not only the *right* way, but ultimately the *only* way to hope and joy. Every knee shall bow and every tongue will confess that gentleness is better than brutality, that kindness is greater than coercion, that the soft voice turneth away wrath" (Conference Report, April 1993, 80).

Blessed are they which do hunger and thirst after
righteousness: for they shall be filled.
—MATTHEW 5:6

When we physically hunger or thirst, we search for food or drink. We know that we cannot live without it. When we earnestly hunger and thirst after righteousness, we can be filled with the Holy Ghost (3 Nephi 12:6). We find the source of everlasting soul satisfaction (2 Nephi 9:51) and feast upon that which never perishes and cannot be corrupted. When we are teachable and soft-hearted, we will be blessed with wisdom, truth, and light which will grow ever brighter (James 3:17; D&C 50:24). Like water and food, the words of eternal life spoken by the Fountain of Living Water and the Bread of Life bring peace, understanding, and salvation. The Savior fills our minds with knowledge, our hearts with comfort, and our souls with joy. Counterfeits of such contentment are everywhere, but, ultimately, nothing else will truly satisfy.

Blessed are the merciful: for they shall obtain mercy.
—MATTHEW 5:7

If we hope to be forgiven, we must forgive. If we want mercy, we must be merciful. A heart without mercy is filled with a gnawing, destructive canker that can eat the soul. The Lord commanded us to "forgive one another; for he that forgiveth not his brother his trespasses standeth condemned before the Lord; for there remaineth in him the greater sin. I, the Lord, will forgive whom I will forgive, but of you it is required to forgive all men" (D&C 64:9–10). A heart can be softened and made merciful by a deep love and appreciation for the Savior and his atonement. Prayer and repentance can transform grieving, angry hearts into compassionate hearts. The effort to forgive others is small compared to the greatness of the profound peace and lasting love awaiting those who impart mercy. Our extending mercy is in similitude of God's offering mercy to all who come unto him.

Blessed are the pure in heart: for they shall see God.
—MATTHEW 5:8

The pure in heart—those who deny themselves of ungodliness and worldly lusts, who forsake their sins, come unto Christ, call on his name, and obey his voice—are those whose eye is single to God's work and glory (JST Matthew 16:26; D&C 88:67; 93:1). They will see God, for they perceive spiritual realities not discernible to the worldly. The Savior says, "Inasmuch as you strip yourselves from jealousies and fears, and humble yourselves before me, for ye are not sufficiently humble, the veil shall be rent and you shall see me and know that I am—not with the carnal neither natural mind, but with the spiritual" (D&C 67:10). Such transcendent privileges are not granted to satisfy whims or curiosity; rather, the Lord Omniscient, who knows best our capacity, will bring this promise to pass "in his own time, and in his own way, and according to his own will" (D&C 88:68).

Blessed are the peacemakers:
for they shall be called the children of God.
—MATTHEW 5:9

The gospel is a message of peace to all people. Blessed are those who make peace amidst turmoil. Fortunate are those who feel contentment even in troubled times. Happy are those who seek reconciliation with God and man. Peace requires deep faith in God and in life. Peace takes patience and practice, effort and energy. Peace comes from humbly doing our best, turning our hearts to God, and following his commands. The psalmist said, "Do good; seek peace" (Psalm 34:14). When we do good, we find peace. When we are truly at peace, we reach out to others in love. May we spread peace throughout the world—one heart at a time—by seeking for peace within ourselves and by giving goodness to others.

Blessed are they which are persecuted for righteousness' sake:
for theirs is the kingdom of heaven.
—MATTHEW 5:10

All true disciples witness that salvation comes only through accepting Jesus Christ and his covenants and ordinances, for his is the only name under heaven whereby salvation can come (2 Nephi 25:20; D&C 18:21–28). During this mortal probation, we may be persecuted and reviled for Jesus' sake, but if we keep our covenants and endure well, God will exalt us on high (D&C 121:8, 29). "Whoso layeth down his life in my cause, for my name's sake, shall find it again, even life eternal" (D&C 98:13). While in Liberty Jail, the Prophet wrote under inspiration: "The Son of Man hath descended below them all. Art thou greater than he? Therefore, hold on thy way. . . . Thy days are known, and thy years shall not be numbered less; therefore, fear not what man can do, for God shall be with you forever and ever" (D&C 122:8–9).

*Ye are the salt of the earth: but if the salt have lost his savour,
wherewith shall it be salted? it is thenceforth good for nothing,
but to be cast out, and to be trodden under foot of men.*
—MATTHEW 5:13

The followers of Christ are capable of making a difference in the world to the degree that they are truly different from the worldly. The people of the Lord, those who have come out of the world by covenant (D&C 101:39–40), are empowered to bring out the best in others. As salt preserves food from corruption and keeps it wholesome and acceptable, so the covenant people are called to stand as witnesses against creeping relativism and the dilution of time-honored values. In this sense, the people of God are called to be saviors of men (D&C 103:9–10). Such influence for good is both timely and timeless. Salt loses its savor not with age but through mixture and contamination. Thus the Master invites his followers to participate in pure religion, to "keep [themselves] unspotted from the vices of the world" (JST James 1:27).

*Ye are the light of the world. . . . Let your light so shine
before men, that they may see your good works,
and glorify your Father which is in heaven.*
—MATTHEW 5:14–16

A former director of the Brigham Young University
Jerusalem Center, while negotiating with religious and
political leaders to establish the Center, gave assur-
ances that the students would not proselytize. One
civic leader quickly countered, "What will we do about
the light in their eyes?" He had met several BYU students, and he knew their light could not be hidden.
Whenever we reflect the Savior's light, we glorify our
Father in Heaven. His light illuminates our being. The
more we strive to walk the path of righteousness, the
more his light shines forth from us and the more
recognizable it becomes to others. The risen Lord
declared: "Behold I am the light; I have set an example
for you. . . . Hold up your light that it may shine
unto the world. Behold I am the light which ye shall
hold up—that which ye have seen me do" (3 Nephi
18:16–24).

FEBRUARY 28

*For I say unto you, That except your righteousness shall
exceed the righteousness of the scribes and Pharisees,
ye shall in no case enter into the kingdom of heaven.*
—MATTHEW 5:20

In the days of Jesus, the Pharisees considered themselves a step above others in their observance of religious practices and ritual. They "trusted in themselves
that they were righteous, and despised others" (Luke
18:9). They determined their own goodness and
measured their own faithfulness by the degree to
which they paid their tithes and offerings, observed
the Sabbath, and kept themselves aloof from ritually
unclean persons or circumstances. Jesus taught,
"There is none good but one, that is, God" (Matthew
19:17). God, not man, sets standards of right and
wrong. People who are "ignorant of God's righteousness" go about seeking to "establish their own
righteousness" (Romans 10:3). Unless we can keep the
law of God more thoroughly than do those who claim
to live it perfectly, we would do well to trust in the
mercy and grace of the one truly perfect Being.

MARCH

I am the good shepherd,
and know my sheep,
and am known of mine.
—JOHN 10:14

*Ye have heard that it was said by them of old time, Thou shalt not
kill; . . . but I say unto you, That whosoever is angry with his
brother without a cause shall be in danger of the judgment.*
—MATTHEW 5:21–22

The phrase "without a cause" found in Matthew 5:22 in the King James Version is omitted from many of the oldest biblical manuscripts and from the Savior's sermon to the Nephites at the temple in Bountiful. Anger, a secondary emotion and a reactionary one, is not an acceptable emotion. It is not inspired of God, does not build relationships, and seldom solves problems. Rather, it builds walls between people, nurtures resentments, and stifles the flow of the pure love of Christ. President David O. McKay declared: "Never must there be expressed in a Latter-day Saint home an oath, a condemnatory term, an expression of anger or jealousy or hatred. Control it! Do not express it! You do what you can to produce peace and harmony, no matter what you may suffer. The Savior set the example. He was always calm, always controlled, radiating something which people could feel as they passed" (*Man May Know for Himself,* 110).

Ye have heard that it was said by them of old time,
Thou shalt not commit adultery: But I say unto you, That
whosoever looketh on a woman to lust after her hath committed
adultery with her already in her heart.
—MATTHEW 5:27 28

The Lord declared in modern revelation, "He that looketh upon a woman to lust after her shall deny the faith, and shall not have the Spirit; and if he repents not he shall be cast out" (D&C 42:23). "Was there ever adultery without dishonesty?" asks President Gordon B. Hinckley. "In the vernacular, the evil is described as 'cheating.' And cheating it is, for it robs virtue, it robs loyalty, it robs sacred promises, it robs self-respect, it robs truth. It involves deception. It is personal dishonesty of the worst kind, for it becomes a betrayal of the most sacred of human relationships and a denial of covenants and promises entered into before God and man. It is the sordid violation of a trust. It is a selfish casting aside of the law of God, and like other forms of dishonesty its fruits are sorrow, bitterness, heartbroken companions, and betrayed children" (*Teachings of Gordon B. Hinckley*, 5).

If thy right eye offend thee, pluck it out, and cast it from thee. . . .
And if thy right hand offend thee, cut it off, and cast it from thee.
—MATTHEW 5:29–30

The Savior directs us to cut off the worldly elements of our nature—persons, places, character defects, or specific sins—that get in the way of our own or others' spiritual progress. Alma taught his errant son, Corianton: "Repent and forsake your sins, and go no more after the lusts of your eyes, but *cross yourself* in all these things; for except ye do this ye can in nowise inherit the kingdom of God" (Alma 39:9; italics added). The unusual phrase "cross yourself" seems to be a loving father's call to his son to take up his cross and deny himself of ungodliness and worldly lusts (JST Matthew 16:26; Mosiah 3:19). The Joseph Smith Translation adds these crucial words to the Master's charge recorded in Matthew: "Now this I speak, a parable concerning your sins; wherefore, cast them from you, that ye may not be hewn down and cast into the fire" (JST Matthew 5:34).

It hath been said by them of old time, Thou shalt not forswear
thyself . . . : But I say unto you, Swear not at all. . . .
But let your communication be, Yea, yea; Nay, nay:
for whatsoever is more than these cometh of evil.
—MATTHEW 5: 33–37

The law of Moses required the taking of oaths as a formal part of religious life (Numbers 30:2). Jesus fulfilled all of the law of Moses, including the part that required the taking of oaths. Elder Bruce R. McConkie wrote: "Beginning in the meridian of time, Jesus revealed a higher standard relative to truthfulness in conversation. It was simply that Yea meant Yea, and Nay meant Nay, and that no oath was required to establish the verity of any promise or thing. Every man's every word was to be as true and accurate as if it had been spoken with an oath. . . . Christ's law assumes that man will keep his word without an oath. If every man were perfectly honest it would not be necessary to take oaths in court or to prepare affidavits and other sworn statements to prove controversial matters" (*Doctrinal New Testament Commentary*, 1:226–27).

Whosoever shall smite thee on thy right cheek, turn to him
the other also. And if any man will sue thee at the law,
and take away thy coat, let him have thy cloke also.
—MATTHEW 5:39–40

Christian discipleship does not entail becoming a nonentity, a person so eager to please that he simply gives himself over to the wishes and whims of those about him. Jesus was certainly not a weakling, nor are his disciples called to be. Followers of Christ are called to be a dynamic influence for good, a power of righteousness in a world with fading values. At the same time, the Christian does not need to be in control of every discussion or correct in every disagreement. Sometimes there are things that matter even more than being right. Confrontation and dispute and debate are not always necessary. The follower of the Prince of Peace is perfectly willing to let some things go.

*Ye have heard that it hath been said, Thou shalt love thy
neighbour, and hate thine enemy. But I say unto you,
Love your enemies, bless them that curse you,
do good to them that hate you, and pray for them
which despitefully use you, and persecute you.*
—MATTHEW 5:43–44

Jesus emphasized the fulness of the law of love: love everyone, especially those whom we might not be disposed to love. Consider the example of Enos in the Book of Mormon. Enos felt remorse for his sins and prayed in mighty supplication for his soul. But he didn't stop there. He prayed for the welfare of his brethren, his loved ones. Then he prayed for his enemies, the Lamanites. With ever-widening reach, his heart turned outward in prayer, and he received promises for all. That is Christ's gospel law of love. The Savior shows the nature of God's perfect love when he reminds us that our Father in Heaven "maketh his sun to rise on the evil and on the good, and sendeth rain on the just and on the unjust" (Matthew 5:45). God's love depends not upon our righteousness but upon his. He extends his love to all who will receive it.

Ye are therefore commanded to be perfect,
even as your Father who is in heaven is perfect.
—JST MATTHEW 5:50

The commandment to be perfect takes our breath away, spiritually speaking, teaching us that we cannot lower the standard held out to the followers of the Christ. Rather, our task is to view our challenge with perspective, to see things as they really are and as they really will be. The Lord Jesus Christ—the only one who has led a perfect life, doing all things right and never taking a moral detour or a backward step—calls upon us to lean upon him and his perfection as we do our best to become like him. Thus we become perfect *in Christ:* We have confidence in him, rely upon his mercy, and trust in his redeeming grace. Those who inherit the highest heaven are "just men [and women] made perfect through Jesus the mediator of the new covenant, who wrought out this perfect atonement through the shedding of his own blood" (D&C 76:69).

Be ye therefore merciful, as your Father also is merciful.
—LUKE 6:36

In God's great plan for his children's happiness, "God himself [Jesus Christ] atoneth for the sins of the world, to bring about the plan of mercy, to appease the demands of justice, that God might be a perfect, just God, and a merciful God also" (Alma 42:15). Mercifully, the Father sent his Son and the Son laid down his life that we might have immortality and eternal life. As we experience the infinite love that redeems us and the transcendent hope that comes from forgiveness, divine love fills our hearts and we want to share this love, hope, and forgiveness with others. Elder Dallin H. Oaks taught, "Forgiveness is mortality's mirror image of the mercy of God" (*Ensign,* November 1989, 66). Thankfully, life is a process of growth, and the more clearly we recognize our own need for mercy, the more merciful we become.

And when thou prayest, thou shalt not be as the hypocrites are:
for they love to pray standing in the synagogues and in the
corners of the streets, that they may be seen of men.
Verily I say unto you, They have their reward.
—MATTHEW 6:5

The prayer of a child, unadorned and without pretense, is a most sublime expression. If we are to become as a child in order to enter the kingdom of God, we must approach in our own prayers the simple entreaties of a child. A two-year-old, expressing the deepest desire of his heart, included the words, "Help us to be happy" each time he prayed. An elderly man commented that his prayers are now more often expressions of gratitude than requests. Whether we are two or eighty-two, prayer is an expression of our heart, a reflection of our relationship with heaven. Public prayer is not for sermonizing but for offering expressions of gratitude and supplication. True disciples are less concerned with eloquence and more concerned with communing with God, less interested in selecting just the right words to impress and more influenced by a humble attitude in which to petition our Maker.

Moreover when ye fast, be not, as the hypocrites, of a sad countenance: for they disfigure their faces, that they may appear unto men to fast. Verily I say unto you, They have their reward.
—MATTHEW 6:16

President Joseph F. Smith taught that "the aim in fasting is to secure perfect purity of heart and simplicity of intention—a fasting unto God in the fullest and deepest sense—for such a fast would be a cure for every practical and intellectual error; vanity would disappear, love for our fellows would take its place, and we would gladly assist the poor and the needy" (*Joseph F. Smith,* 198). Communion with the Infinite increases as we transcend the flesh through fasting to reach a heightened spirituality. Fasting accompanied by prayer (Alma 17:3) increases the earnestness of our supplications, opens our hearts to the things of eternity, and invites humility as we are reminded of our dependence on God. The fast-day plan of the Lord is the practical provision God has made in his Church to care for those in need. We fast, we pray, and we give our offering of money and a willing heart to the Lord.

Lay up for yourselves treasures in heaven, where neither moth nor rust doth corrupt, and where thieves do not break through nor steal: For where your treasure is, there will your heart be also.
—MATTHEW 6:20–21

Money and all that it buys, prestige and all that it brings, position and all that it bestows—all these end at death's door. But we can lay up treasures in heaven. Righteous acts, sincere service, and genuine love add to our eternal treasure account. Character developed by keeping covenants and humble submission to the divine will add to our account. Knowledge, faith, mercy, and truth are among the godly attributes that can go with us into immortality (Alma 41:13–15). Those with the most magnificent treasures in heaven will be those who simply went about doing good, who loved and served, whose spirituality was deep down inside and largely unheralded. Treasures of earth inevitably disappear in time. Those whose righteousness is authentic, who conscientiously help others, who truly have his name written in their hearts gain the greatest treasure of all—eternal life in the kingdom of God.

The light of the body is the eye; if therefore thine eye be single to the glory of God, thy whole body shall be full of light.
—JST MATTHEW 6:22

God's work and glory is to "bring to pass the immortality and eternal life of man" (Moses 1:39). To have an eye single to that glory is to have our mind and heart riveted on that enterprise—to be fully committed to, thoroughly focused on, and absolutely driven by that overarching and undergirding labor. It is to have put aside selfish ambition and competing allegiances, to have chosen first things first. As someone has wisely observed, if we have chosen something other than the kingdom of God first, it will make little difference in the end what we have chosen instead. While this way is strait and narrow, the reward is glorious: "And if your eye be single to my glory, your whole bodies shall be filled with light, and there shall be no darkness in you; and that body which is filled with light comprehendeth all things" (D&C 88:67).

No man can serve two masters: for either he will hate the one,
and love the other; or else he will hold to the one,
and despise the other. Ye cannot serve God and mammon.
—MATTHEW 6:24

*M*ammon, an Aramaic word meaning "riches," can be anything—ego, laziness, selfishness, deceptive teachers, worldly preoccupations, habits—that leads us away from the Master. The world offers false gods that tempt us to loosen our grip on the iron rod. Promises of immediate and visible rewards may make it seem easier to serve mammon, but his rewards are fleeting and fatiguing. We tire of them, always needing more to stay satisfied. God's rewards, on the other hand, are refreshing, invigorating, and lasting. With a wide-angle view of eternal things and a Spirit-enhanced depth perception of the things that matter most, we can see mammon's lures for what they are. But we lose sight of eternal rewards whenever we waver from a whole-souled commitment to God. Our complete loyalty to the true Master grows in response to the love, peace, and joy we feel as we follow him.

Take no thought for your life, what ye shall eat, or what ye shall drink; nor yet for your body, what ye shall put on. Is not the life more than meat, and the body than raiment?
—MATTHEW 6:25

We have been counseled to live in the present, to enjoy today all that is virtuous, lovely, and of good report (Articles of Faith 1:13). We have also been counseled to live providently, to set reasonable goals for ourselves, and to do some long-range planning. In truth, we must look to the future without becoming obsessed by it, and we must live *now*. Remember that Jesus' words in Matthew 6:25 were delivered primarily to the Twelve, men who were to go into the world without purse or scrip as full-time ministers of the gospel. And "take no thought" does not mean "don't think about" but rather "don't be overly anxious about." Of course, we should put aside something for a rainy day, but the Lord does not want us to become so focused on our future holdings that they hold us hostage. We must not be possessed by our possessions, whether now or thirty years from now.

Wherefore, seek not the things of this world but seek ye first to build up the kingdom of God, and to establish his righteousness, and all these things shall be added unto you.
—JST MATTHEW 6:38

The Savior's call to a higher righteousness includes a purification of our motives, a cleansing of our heart and desires. As Christians we are called to do the right thing and to do it for the right reason. "We must put God in the forefront of everything else in our lives," President Ezra Taft Benson counseled us. "He must come first, just as He declares in the first of His Ten Commandments. . . . When we put God first, all other things fall into their proper place or drop out of our lives. Our love of the Lord will govern the claims for our affection, the demands on our time, the interests we pursue, and the order of our priorities" (*Ensign,* May 1988, 4).

Judge not unrighteously, that ye be not judged;
but judge righteous judgment.
—JST MATTHEW 7:2

As men and women seeking to be holy, we are obliged to make judgments every day. We must decide whether we will spend time with this person or another, in this place or that, doing this activity or that. These decisions are part of making our way safely through the mists of darkness; indeed, our hope for eternal life depends upon our judging righteously. Of course, we must be understanding, loving, and concerned, but these virtues must never cloud the issue of right and wrong, good and evil. We must not allow Christian tolerance to be used as the means of making vice acceptable. Yet we must avoid condemning others, attributing evil motives to them, or concluding that they are forever lost (or saved). None of us has the requisite data to suggest the eternal destination of one of our brothers or sisters. Such matters must be left to God, who has all knowledge.

And why beholdest thou the mote that is in thy brother's eye,
but considerest not the beam that is in thine own eye?
—MATTHEW 7:3

The only cure for the mote-beam disease is charity. Elder Marvin J. Ashton observed: "Perhaps the greatest charity comes when we are kind to each other, when we don't judge or categorize someone else, when we simply give each other the benefit of the doubt or remain quiet. Charity is accepting someone's differences, weaknesses, and shortcomings; having patience with someone who has let us down; or resisting the impulse to become offended when someone doesn't handle something the way we might have hoped. Charity is refusing to take advantage of another's weakness and being willing to forgive someone who has hurt us. Charity is expecting the best of each other. . . . If we could look into each other's hearts and understand the unique challenges each of us face, I think we would treat each other much more gently, with more love, patience, tolerance, and care" (*Ensign*, May 1992, 19–20).

Give not that which is holy unto the dogs, neither cast ye your pearls before swine, lest they trample them under their feet, and turn again and rend you.
—MATTHEW 7:6

The Lord Jesus Christ was not referring to people as dogs or pigs in Matthew 7:6. Rather, he was declaring that gospel prerequisites should be observed when we are teaching or learning sacred things. A person who knows little about our doctrine will probably not appreciate our beliefs concerning temples, sealing powers, eternal life, or the deification of man. Elder Boyd K. Packer explained that "teaching prematurely or at the wrong time some things that are true can invite sorrow and heartbreak instead of the joy intended to accompany learning. . . . The scriptures teach emphatically that we must give milk before meat. The Lord made it very clear that some things are to be taught selectively, and some things are to be given only to those who are worthy. It matters very much not only what we are told but when we are told it" (*Let Not Your Heart Be Troubled*, 107–8).

Ask, and it shall be given you; seek, and ye shall find; knock,
and it shall be opened unto you: For every one that
asketh receiveth; and he that seeketh findeth;
and to him that knocketh it shall be opened.
—MATTHEW 7:7–8

Ask. *Seek. Knock.* Three words that open the windows of heaven to revelation, problem-solving, consolation, and peace. Three words that seem so simple and yet like many simple things are rarely easy. All three words require action. *Ask.* We have a need, and so we inquire. We cannot receive answers if, through pride or apathy, we fail to ask questions. *Seek.* Life is a quest for solutions, for understanding, for comfort, for guidance through life's turbulent waters. Seeking a safe harbor will lead us to the Comforter, who gives the only real comfort and lasting peace. *Knock.* If we knock with humility and real intent, doors will be opened to us: doors of discernment and peace, doors with answers to life's difficult questions, doors of reconciliation and renewal. In a sense, when we do one of these, we do all three. *Ask. Seek. Knock.* The things of eternity will be opened to us.

Therefore all things whatsoever ye would that men should do to you, do ye even so to them: for this is the law and the prophets.
—MATTHEW 7:12

Perhaps the best-known teaching of Jesus is the Golden Rule. It echoes down through the centuries as the supreme law of living: (Treat others the way you want to be treated) This simple expression contains the secret of how to succeed with people, the ultimate message of meaningful human relations, and the quintessential statement on extending kindness and courtesy to others. Indeed, we might wonder just how different this world would be if people lived their lives according to this grand imperative. What would happen to the hungry and the needy? What would become of warring nations? What scientific and technological progress could be made, what wonders could be worked, if we simply treated others as we desire to be treated?

Strait is the gate, and narrow is the way,
which leadeth unto life, and few there be that find it.
—MATTHEW 7:14

The gate is *strait,* meaning narrow and limited, not *straight* as in a line. By entering in that restricted gate, we get onto the path that leads to eternal life, the kind of life that God lives. Repentance and baptism are the strait gate that we must enter. Keeping the commandments keeps us on the narrow path. Celestial marriage is the strait gate that directs us toward exaltation in the highest heaven. All of these keep us from spiritual death, or hell. "After ye have gotten into this strait and narrow path, I would ask if all is done? Behold, I say unto you, Nay; for ye have not come thus far save it were by the word of Christ. . . . Wherefore, if ye shall press forward, feasting upon the word of Christ, and endure to the end, behold, thus saith the Father: Ye shall have eternal life" (2 Nephi 31:19–20).

*Beware of false prophets, which come to you in
sheep's clothing, but inwardly they are ravening wolves.
Ye shall know them by their fruits.*
—MATTHEW 7:15–16

Years ago an article in a prominent Christian magazine gave several reasons why people were joining the Church, including the following: the Latter-day Saints show genuine love and concern by taking care of their people, they build the family unit, they provide for their young people, and they believe that divine revelation is the basis for their practices. The author concluded: "In a day when many are hesitant to claim that God has said anything definitive, the Mormons stand out in contrast. . . . People are many times ready to hear a voice of authority" ("Why Your Neighbor Joined the Mormon Church," *Christianity Today,* 11 October 1974, 11–13). The Savior taught that "every plant, which my heavenly Father hath not planted, shall be rooted up" (Matthew 15:13). Evil trees cannot bring forth good fruit. Works of men eventually come to naught, but that which is of God cannot be overthrown.

Not every one that saith unto me, Lord, Lord, shall enter into the
kingdom of heaven.... And then [at the day of judgment]
will I profess unto them, I never knew you:
depart from me, ye that work iniquity.
—MATTHEW 7:21–23

True faith, which is faith unto life and salvation, is always manifested in faithful actions. As the apostle James wrote, "Faith without works is dead" (James 2:20). Our profession of faith in the Lord Jesus Christ must be reflected in our daily walk and talk. "If we live in the Spirit," Paul urged, "let us also walk in the Spirit" (Galatians 5:25). Joseph Smith's translation alters the phrase "I never knew you" to "Ye never knew me" (JST Matthew 7:33). Elder Bruce R. McConkie elaborated: "'I [the Lord] never knew you, and you never knew me! . . . Your heart was not so centered in me as to cause you to endure to the end; and so for a time and a season you were faithful; you even worked miracles in my name; but in the end it shall be as though I never knew you'" (*Mortal Messiah*, 2:172–73).

Therefore whosoever heareth these sayings of mine,
and doeth them, I will liken him unto a wise man,
which built his house upon a rock.
—MATTHEW 7:24

The Lord declared, "Build upon my rock, which is my gospel" (D&C 11:24). "This is my doctrine, and whoso buildeth upon this buildeth upon my rock, and the gates of hell shall not prevail against them" (3 Nephi 11:39). Those who build their houses of faith on the rock of revelation, gospel verity, and doctrinal truth will have a fortified structure impervious to every storm, able to withstand any trial or temptation. If we are built on the shifting sands of sectarianism or the mundane matters of this world, however, we will suffer needlessly and eventually will fall. When the rains of adversity come—as they inevitably will—those who have paid the price of spiritual preparation and growth will stand strong against flood, wind, or tempest of every kind. Hearing the words of God is not enough. Only he or she who "doeth them" (Matthew 7:24) is the one who is wise and who is saved.

And it came to pass, when Jesus had ended these sayings,
the people were astonished at his doctrine:
For he taught them as one having authority,
and not as the scribes.
—MATTHEW 7:28–29

Jesus taught the people "as one having authority from God, and not as having authority from the Scribes" (JST Matthew 7:37). Because of his consummate righteousness and his utter dependence upon the Father, what Jesus presented was a message from the Father, and it carried the power of the Father. His words, simple and straightforward, went to the hearts of receptive listeners and burned like fire. Truly, the Master "spake not as other men" (JST Matthew 3:25). Those called to serve in the Lord's kingdom are likewise called to teach with authority from God, not as having been given authority from the scribes of our own day. Christ has charged us to "preach my gospel by the Spirit, even the Comforter which was sent forth to teach the truth. . . . And if it be by some other way it is not of God" (D&C 50:14, 18).

Among those that are born of women there is not a greater
prophet than John the Baptist: but he that is least
in the kingdom of God is greater than he.
—LUKE 7:28

Joseph Smith taught that John the Baptist was the
greatest of all the prophets because "he was entrusted
with a divine mission of preparing the way before the
face of the Lord. . . . It was required at his hands, to
baptize the Son of Man. . . . John, at that time, was the
only legal administrator in the affairs of the kingdom
there was then on the earth." The Prophet added that
Jesus seemingly "was least entitled to their credulity as
a prophet; [it was] as though [Jesus] had said—'He
that is considered the least among you is greater than
John—that is I myself'" (*Teachings of the Prophet Joseph
Smith,* 275–76). John's greatness lay in his doing "none
other things than that which [he was] commanded"
(D&C 132:37). He prepared the people for the Master,
bore witness of the Master, and then stepped aside so
the Master's voice might be heard.

Wherefore I say unto thee, Her sins, which are many,
are forgiven: for she loved much: but to whom
little is forgiven, the same loveth little.
—LUKE 7:47

A deeply contrite and repentant woman who believed in the Savior desired to manifest to him her unbounded gratitude and love beyond measure. Tears dropped upon his feet as she washed them and then wiped them with her hair. In humble submission, she kissed his feet and anointed them with expensive ointment. Both she and the Lord knew how far she had come, how sincere her repentance was, how her heart was broken with remorse and filled with appreciation for the Savior's loving plan of redemption. The Lord knew her heart, extended forgiveness, and sent her away in peace. We bridge the distance between ourselves and the Lord through repentance and gratitude. Little gratitude flows from a hardened heart, but when we have repented and been forgiven of our sins, our heart overflows as we feel to "sing the song of redeeming love" (Alma 5:26).

Out of the abundance of the heart the mouth speaketh.
A good man out of the good treasure of the heart bringeth forth
good things: and an evil man out of the evil
treasure bringeth forth evil things.
—MATTHEW 12:34–35

Individuals with an abundant heart speak well of others, desire the best for all, and reach out in love and service to humankind. Although each of us is far from perfect, if our hearts are good, our actions and attitudes will essentially be good. Those with hard hearts, unforgiving and haughty hearts, produce fruits of bitterness and animosity. Estrangement and distrust are the fruits of those who live with a hard and empty heart. The Prophet Joseph Smith said: "If we would secure and cultivate the love of others, we must love others, even our enemies as well as friends. Sectarian priests cry out concerning me, and ask, 'Why is it this babbler gains so many followers, and retains them?' I answer, It is because I possess the principle of love. All I can offer the world is a good heart and a good hand" (*Teachings of the Prophet Joseph Smith,* 313).

Every idle word that men shall speak,
they shall give account thereof in the day of judgment.
—MATTHEW 12:36

The gospel of Jesus Christ is a call to noble actions and righteous thoughts. It will help us cleanse our hands and purify our thoughts. God commissions each one of us: "Let thine heart keep my commandments" (Proverbs 3:1). Because our thoughts are the seedbeds of our feelings and our deeds, because what we do is so very often a product of our thinking, we face the challenge of elevating our thoughts above the low and beggarly elements of this telestial world. It is true, as President David O. McKay taught, that "what a man continually thinks about determines his actions in times of opportunity and stress" (Conference Report, October 1951, 8). President McKay said further, "I will know what you are if you tell me what you think about when you don't have to think" (*True to the Faith,* 270).

An evil and adulterous generation seeketh after a sign.
—MATTHEW 12:39

How does a disposition to seek after signs relate to seeking after carnal pleasures? Simply stated, those who have given themselves up to their lusts, who have exhausted their passions in their search for the sensual, also seek for physical manifestations of spiritual realities. They demand proof! Refusing to acknowledge eternal certainties, they insist that unfamiliar spiritual truths be translated into that realm they have come to know more fully than any other—the physical. The adulterous are those who worship at the altar of appetite, whose thresholds for gratification are ever rising, and who therefore demand something extraordinary to establish the truthfulness of a claim. Ironically, eternal truth may be verified only by the quiet and unobtrusive whisperings of the Spirit. Spiritual blindness and the spirit of adultery are thus common companions.

A sower went forth to sow; and when he sowed, some seeds fell
by the way side. . . . Some fell upon stony places, where they
had not much earth. . . . And some fell among thorns. . . .
But other fell into good ground, and brought forth fruit.
—MATTHEW 13:3–8

The parable of the sower might well be called the parable of the soils, because it says even more about the soil onto which the word of truth falls than it does about the sower of the word. When a seed falls by the wayside, the word is received but the hearer fails to understand it. When the word is sown on stony ground, the individual declines to involve himself in the labors that would send his spiritual roots deep into the faith. When the word is planted among thorns, the individual refuses to turn away from worldly enticements. But when the seed is planted in good soil and properly nurtured, the harvest is satisfying and the fruits are sweet. This parable encourages us to humbly receive the truth, cherish it, and sink our spiritual roots deep so that neither the pressure of persecution nor the cares of this temporal world can distract us from eternal things.

APRIL

*Jesus took bread, and blessed it, and brake it, and
gave it to the disciples, and said, Take, eat; this is
my body. And he took the cup, and gave thanks,
and gave it to them, saying, Drink ye all of it;
for this is my blood of the new testament, which
is shed for many for the remission of sins.*

—Matthew 26:26–28

The disciples came, and said unto him, Why speakest thou unto
them in parables? He answered, . . . Because it is given
unto you to know the mysteries of the kingdom of heaven,
but to them it is not given.
—MATTHEW 13:10–11

Jesus was the Master Teacher. His teaching methods
were simple: he asked questions, quoted scripture,
made comparisons and contrasts, and drew upon
everyday events or objects to make his points. But the
teaching technique for which he is most well known is
the parable. Parables are stories that teach important
truths. They are imaginary, although the events
described in them could have happened. The parables
of Jesus contain counsel for gaining greater happiness,
warnings, condemnations of hypocrisy, and invitations
to repent and improve. Because Jesus employed parables with both his followers and his enemies, some of
the messages are crystal clear, while others are inten-
tionally veiled. Jesus explained, "Unto you that believe
not, I speak in parables; that your unrighteousness may
be rewarded unto you" (JST Matthew 21:34). The
simplicity or complexity of the parable thus depends
upon the spiritual receptivity of those who hear it.

*And he said, So is the kingdom of God, as if a man should cast seed
into the ground; and should sleep, and rise night and day,
and the seed should spring and grow up, he knoweth not how.*
—MARK 4:26–27

The parable of the fruit-bearing earth, found only
in the Gospel of Mark, is somewhat different from the
other parables of the kingdom in Matthew 13. Those
parables focus on such virtues as receptivity, produc-
tivity, and vigilance. This parable of the fruit-bearing
earth points us toward another profound truth. We as
disciples may receive and treasure the word and do all
in our power to cultivate the soil into which the seed is
sown, yet spiritual growth and transformation of the
soul are generous gifts from the Father of Lights. In
chastening the Corinthian Saints for their tendency
to create schisms in the Church by identifying with
this Church leader or that one, Paul asked, "Who then
is Paul, and who is Apollos, but ministers by whom ye
believed, even as the Lord gave to every man? I have
planted, Apollos watered; but God gave the increase"
(1 Corinthians 3:5–6).

I will say to the reapers, Gather ye together first the tares,
and bind them in bundles to burn them:
but gather the wheat into my barn.
—MATTHEW 13:30

The Savior's parable of the wheat and the tares powerfully illustrates the establishment of the Church in our day, the wickedness of the world, and the day of harvest at the end of the world when the Church and the earth will be cleansed and the wicked destroyed (D&C 86:1–7). This parable is both an explanation and warning. The tares planted by the adversary grow side by side with the wheat, but the forces of evil around us will not overtake us if we plant our hearts deep in gospel soil. We need not be afraid of the tares, but we must stand firm and "pray always lest that wicked one have power in you, and remove you out of your place" (D&C 93:49). Now is the time to decide whether we will be burned with the tares or gathered with the wheat to receive eternal life.

The kingdom of heaven is like to a grain of mustard seed, . . .
which . . . is the least of all seeds: but when it is grown,
it is the greatest among herbs, and becometh a tree,
so that the birds of the air come and lodge in the branches.
—MATTHEW 13: 31–32

The Prophet Joseph said: "Let us take the Book of Mormon, which a man took and hid in his field, securing it by his faith, to spring up in the last days, or in due time; let us behold it coming forth out of the ground, which is indeed accounted the least of all seeds; but behold it branching forth, yea, even towering, with lofty branches, and God-like majesty, until it, like the mustard seed, becomes the greatest of all herbs. And . . . God is sending down His powers, gifts and angels, to lodge in the branches thereof" (*Teachings of the Prophet Joseph Smith,* 98). Like the stone cut without hands whose rolling forth cannot be stopped (Daniel 2; D&C 65), The Church of Jesus Christ of Latter-day Saints will grow until "the earth shall be full of the knowledge of the Lord, as the waters cover the sea" (Isaiah 11:9).

*Another parable spake he unto them; The kingdom of heaven
is like unto leaven, which a woman took,
and hid in three measures of meal,
till the whole was leavened.*
—MATTHEW 13:33

The Saints are called to be the leaven in the loaf of the world, that small but powerful influence that fosters growth, change, and development. "Leaven was a piece of last week's dough, which certainly made this week's dough rise. . . . The leaven was but a small amount, but in time it changed the large quantity of flour." This parable "brings out the contrast and the continuity between the small beginnings of the kingdom and its great consummation. The little group of disciples might be despised as preaching a kingdom too insignificant to be noticed, but as surely as a tiny piece of leaven had its effect on a large mass of dough, so surely would the kingdom have its effect throughout the world" (Morris, *Gospel According to Matthew,* 353). In short, the people of the covenant are put in place by an all-wise Creator to make their influence felt— to make a difference.

The kingdom of heaven is like unto treasure hid in a field;
the which when a man hath found, he hideth,
and for joy thereof goeth and selleth all
that he hath, and buyeth that field.
—MATTHEW 13:44

Some go in search of the treasure of the gospel, and others, like the man in the parable of the treasure hid in the field, almost seem to stumble onto it. But how we come to the gospel is not so important as what we do with the treasure once we've found it. In the parable, the man sells all that he has to obtain the treasure. Clearly, the gospel itself is not for sale, and yet the gospel treasure is the greatest gift we can receive. Everything else is dross compared to the riches of Christ. When we truly embrace the gospel covenant, forsake worldly things, and follow the Savior, we begin a new life. We sincerely strive to give away all our smallness and selfishness, wicked desires and unholy intentions, pride and self-aggrandizement, that we might enjoy the treasures of eternity.

There arose a great tempest in the sea, . . . and his
disciples came to him, and awoke him, saying, Lord,
save us: we perish. . . . Then he arose, and rebuked
the winds and the sea; and there was a great calm.
—MATTHEW 8:24–26

No one can escape this life without encountering some measure of opposition, tragedy, or irony. It's all part of life, yet often we cry out in agony, "Why is this happening to me?" The truthful answer is, Because we're mortal. We agreed to these conditions—even the painful and uncomfortable ones—long before we were born. Far more productive are such questions as "What should I learn from this?" or "How can I use this suffering to bless others?" or even "Where can I turn for help?" If we seek his guidance and comfort, the Pilot of our ship, he who guides our craft through life's tempestuous seas, will see us safely to our eternal home.

*And Jesus said, Somebody hath touched me. . . . And when the
woman saw that she was not hid, she came trembling, and
falling down before him, she declared unto him . . .
how she was healed immediately. And he said
unto her, . . . thy faith hath made thee whole.*
—LUKE 8:46–48

U ltimately, faith in the Lord Jesus Christ is the
source of spiritual and physical healing. As the divine
Healer affirmed, the woman who had been hemor-
rhaging for a dozen years exercised great faith in the
Lord. She was endowed with one of the gifts of the
Spirit, "faith to be healed" (D&C 46:19). With
humble faith, she believed that to touch Jesus would
heal her. The integrity of her heart opened the way for
a healing to take place. Unlike the sick who gathered
by the pool of Bethesda (John 5:1–9), this woman
exercised faith in Jesus Christ. She knew that healing
was to be found in him and in her faith to be healed.
Though today we cannot physically touch the hem of
Christ's garment, we can nevertheless exercise faith.
We can keep the commandments, have hope in his
teachings, and trust in his promises and his power.

And when he was come into his own country,
he taught them in their synagogue. . . . And they were
offended in him. But Jesus said unto them, A prophet
is not without honour, save in his own country.
—MATTHEW 13:54–57

Jesus was the foster son of a carpenter, and Mary was his mother. When he returned to Nazareth of Galilee, where he had lived as a youth, he was not given due respect. Surely his fellow townsmen knew he was no ordinary man. They knew his exceptional parents, yet in their blindness of heart they rejected him. Do we do the same to others? Do we disparage members of our own household or community whom we know well? To be rejected or unappreciated by those closest to us can cause the deepest kind of pain. It is easy to hold in awe people we don't know. A bigger heart is required to love, honor, and understand those we do know well: family, neighbors, other members of our ward and stake, people with whom we regularly associate. To recognize true greatness in these brings out the best in them—and in us.

Jesus said unto them, A prophet is not without honour, but in his own country, and among his own kin, and in his own house.
—MARK 6:4

I s not this the carpenter's son?" skeptics asked in the meridian of time (Matthew 13:55; Mark 6:3). "He's one of us. How could he know so much?" "He's from Nazareth. How could he possibly be the Messiah?" The questions were similar in Joseph Smith's day. "I knew him as a boy—he's from Manchester, isn't he? What right does he have to claim a revelation?" A universal malady has been the inability of people to accept as a prophet one called of God from among themselves. Perhaps the problem is one of unrealistic expectation. Jesus was condemned for eating and drinking with publicans and sinners; surely no deliverer or redeemer would lower himself to affiliate with the dregs of society. Joseph Smith was condemned for joking and wrestling with the boys; certainly a prophet is made of more austere stuff. Prophets are men approved of God—what further and greater recommendation do we need?

These twelve Jesus sent forth, and commanded them,
saying, Go not into the way of the Gentiles,
and into any city of the Samaritans enter ye not:
But go rather to the lost sheep of the house of Israel.
—MATTHEW 10:5–6

God, who knows the end from the beginning, "hath made of one blood all nations of men for to dwell on all the face of the earth, and hath determined the times before appointed, and the bounds of their habitation; that they should seek the Lord, if they are willing to find him, for he is not far from every one of us" (JST Acts 17:26–27). Our Heavenly Father has planned for the spread of his word and the establishment of his kingdom on earth according to his own divine timetable. Truly, the Lord esteems all flesh in one (1 Nephi 17:35) and loves all his children. But the gospel is sent to individuals and nations when the Lord sees fit. In the meridian of time, the gospel went first to the Jews and later to the Gentiles. Now, in the dispensation of the fulness of times, the gospel is going forth to all the world.

Behold, I send you forth as sheep in the midst of wolves:
be ye therefore wise as serpents, and harmless as doves.
—MATTHEW 10:16

Jesus sent forth his apostles to preach the gospel, the good news, to a world in which evil people, "ravening wolves," want nothing more than to thwart the work of the Lord and destroy his kingdom. And while his witnesses are sent to declare boldly his saving truth, they are not to seek persecution or martyrdom or give offense. They are to be forthright, yet respectful; competent, yet guileless; courageous, yet wise. The Joseph Smith Translation adds clarification and insight: "Be ye therefore *wise servants,* and as harmless as doves" (JST Matthew 10:14; italics added). As wise servants, the Lord's agents are to go forth, without returning evil for evil, to carry his message to the world. The Lord's instruction applies to us all. How much more effective are those who are steadfast and strong, yet gentle and without guile. Their influence will reverberate throughout their communities and countries.

Take no thought how or what ye shall speak: for it shall be given you in that same hour what ye shall speak. For it is not ye that speak, but the Spirit of your Father which speaketh in you.
—MATTHEW 10:19–20

Those who hear the testimonies of the servants of God are his children. The Father empowers his servants to speak and act in his name. Their deeds become his deeds, and their words become his words. When they speak by the power of the Holy Ghost, they speak the words of Christ (2 Nephi 32:2–3). If they will "treasure up in [their] minds continually the words of life, . . . it shall be given [them] in the very hour that portion that shall be meted unto every man" (D&C 84:85). The Lord promises his servants: "You shall not be confounded before men; for it shall be given you in the very hour, yea, in the very moment, what ye shall say. . . . Inasmuch as ye do this the Holy Ghost shall be shed forth in bearing record unto all things whatsoever ye shall say" (D&C 100:5–8).

*And fear not them which kill the body, but are not able to
kill the soul: but rather fear him which is able to
destroy both soul and body in hell.*
—MATTHEW 10:28

Through the elevated perspective provided by the Restoration, we understand the purpose of the physical body and the infinite value of mortal life. At the same time, there is something more awful than suffering, something to be dreaded even more than physical death. We recognize that losing a limb or having to function without an eye, though difficult or even tragic, is not as serious as losing one's soul, surrendering one's hope of eternal life. While seeking to avoid persecution or martyrdom, we as true servants of the Master are vigilant and attentive to the sometimes subtle assaults on the soul by the father of all lies. We watch and pray to elude the snares of him who seeks that "all men might be miserable like unto himself" (2 Nephi 2:27).

Think not that I am come to send peace on earth. . . . He that loveth father or mother more than me is not worthy of me: and he that loveth son or daughter more than me is not worthy of me.
—MATTHEW 10: 34–37

The gospel that would have us love our enemies and turn the other cheek requires us to uphold the sword of truth and love God above all else—even family relationships. Certainly, we are not to seek for discord, and often there need not be any. But consider those devout converts who have been forced to make such a decision. Think of those who have left behind family, country, and all else they loved to build the kingdom of God. Many have faced persecution from those they loved most and have even been cut off from association with them in order to seal their testimonies of the gospel. We honor such sacrifices by welcoming the faithful into the fold and doing all in our power to strengthen those who have accepted life-altering truth and chosen Christ and his Church.

And he that taketh not his cross,
and followeth after me, is not worthy of me.
—Matthew 10:38

Christ's foreshadowing the death he will suffer teaches us that we must be willing to surrender our will and give our all to become his disciples. Luke's account adds the phrase, "Let him deny himself, and take up his cross daily, and follow me" (Luke 9:23). We must take up our cross daily, not just occasionally. We take up our cross when we voluntarily submit our will to the Lord. We take up our cross to follow Christ when we endure the sorrows and vicissitudes of life because of our faith in the Savior and the requirements of the plan of salvation. To be the Savior's disciple, we must follow him. We must strive with all our hearts to be like him, to be true to the cause of righteousness. This is an active, vibrant, daily process. We must take up our cross and follow him, neither waiting until he comes to us nor casually observing from a distance.

He who seeketh to save his life shall lose it;
and he who loseth his life for my sake shall find it.
—JST MATTHEW 10:34

The more you obey your conscience," C. S. Lewis observed, "the more your conscience will demand of you. And your natural self, which is thus being starved and hampered and worried at every turn, will get angrier and angrier. It is as though Jesus were saying to each of us: 'Give me All. I don't want so much of your time and so much of your money and so much of your work: I want You. I have not come to torment your natural self, but to kill it. . . . I will give you a new self instead. In fact, I will give you Myself: my own will shall become yours'" (*Mere Christianity,* 169). Those who turn to the Lord and covenant with him travel the path that leads to the abundant life. That life is worth whatever price we are required to pay, and in the end we shall see there really was no sacrifice.

And they went out, and preached that men should repent.
—MARK 6:12

The first elders of the new dispensation were instructed, "Say nothing but repentance unto this generation" (D&C 6:9) and "Preach naught but repentance" (D&C 19:21). John and Peter Whitmer Jr. were told, "The thing which will be of the most worth unto you will be to declare repentance unto this people, that you may bring souls unto me, that you may rest with them in the kingdom of my Father" (D&C 15:6; 16:6). These directives "mean that the Lord's ministers are to confine their teachings to the doctrines of the gospel. They are to teach that gospel repentance which is in effect the very plan of salvation itself" (McConkie, *New Witness,* 220). The call to repent is thus the call to improve, to be refined, to be purified. Indeed, to come unto Christ is to choose to be changed.

*And they say unto him, We have here but five loaves, and two
fishes. He said, Bring them hither to me. . . . And they did all
eat, . . . and they took up of the fragments that remained
twelve baskets full. And they that had eaten were about
five thousand men, beside women and children.*
—MATTHEW 14: 17–21

It should not surprise us that the Great Jehovah, who created worlds without end, has the power to feed several thousand people with five loaves and two fishes. The Fountain of Living Water could certainly feed their bodies and prepare their spirits for the transcendent truths he would impart in his sermon on the Bread of Life. This miraculous act both fed the hungry and witnessed to them that Jesus was indeed the Son of God. It was a prelude of the spiritual feast that would follow. Although it is beyond our finite capacity to comprehend how this act of love was performed, we know the Master loves us and desires to fill our souls with the bread of eternal life. All things are possible to him who is our Lord.

When Jesus therefore perceived that they would come and take
him by force, to make him a king, he departed again
into a mountain himself alone.
—JOHN 6:15

The Master declared to Pilate, "My kingdom is not of this world" (John 18:36). Jesus did not come to earth to be crowned king by mortals. He did not heal the sick, raise the dead, or demonstrate power over the elements to elicit cheers and praise from the crowds. He came to do the will of the Father—to call people to repentance, to point them to the truth and toward truthful living, and to lay down his life as a willing sacrifice for the salvation of all humankind. Whether he was liked, whether he was popular, whether others placed him high on society's list of those "most likely to succeed" did not concern him. He had a work to do, a sublime work that mortals could not fathom.

Peter . . . walked on the water, to go to Jesus. But when he saw the
wind boisterous, he was afraid; and beginning to sink,
he cried, saying, Lord save me. And immediately
Jesus stretched forth his hand, and caught him.
—MATTHEW 14:29–31

As long as Peter fixed his gaze on the Savior, he was able to do what was thought impossible. The instant his focus shifted to the heavy wind, he began to sink. Some might say Peter failed, but this is a great lesson in faith. Peter did indeed walk on the water, but even when he became afraid, he knew where to look for salvation. In calling upon the Savior to rescue him, he continued to exercise faith. Clearly, he had faith the Savior would bring him safely to the ship. Whatever winds of adversity may beset us, when we sincerely seek Jesus, he will bring us safely home. We may be asked to try uncertain waters, we may be expected to face strong winds of discouragement and doubt, but if we persist, he will increase our faith and rescue our souls.

And whithersoever he entered, into villages, or cities, or country,
they laid the sick in the streets, and besought him that they
might touch if it were but the border of his garment:
and as many as touched him were made whole.
MARK 6:56

Although many touched the hem of Jesus' garment, the power to be healed was not in the garment. It was not in the clay that the blind man was instructed to put over his eyes and then wash away (John 9:6). The power resided within the Lord himself—and in those who had faith in him. As people looked to the Savior, heard his words, believed his witness, trusted him, and exercised faith and hope in him, miracles took place in their lives. Sometimes their hearts were touched and their souls transformed. Sometimes their broken bodies were mended. Always an encounter with Jesus on the part of a believer is a lifting, liberating, life-changing experience. We are never the same after we come unto Christ.

And Jesus said unto them, I am the bread of life:
he that cometh to me shall never hunger;
and he that believeth on me shall never thirst.
—JOHN 6:35

When the multitude wanted bread from heaven, Jesus testified that he is the living manna, the sustainer of his covenant people. "The bread of God is he which cometh down from heaven, and giveth life unto the world" (John 6:33). When the multitude clamored, "Give us this bread," Jesus declared, "I am the bread of life" (John 6:34–35). Jesus offers himself to all as the source of temporal and spiritual happiness, for it is he who forgives his people, leads them out of spiritual bondage, and feeds their souls. Manna was sent from heaven to feed the children of Israel in similitude of Christ's coming to earth as the true bread of life. Likewise, when we partake of the sacramental bread, we symbolically make the Savior a part of ourselves. He is our source of spiritual sustenance and our only and everlasting hope of deliverance from the bondage of the world.

Verily, verily, I say unto you,
He that believeth on me hath everlasting life.
—JOHN 6:47

The Philippian jailer asked the apostle Paul, "What must I do to be saved?" Paul answered, "Believe on the Lord Jesus Christ, and thou shalt be saved, and thy house" (Acts 16:30–31). To believe on Christ is to believe that he is God's Almighty Son, that he was called and prepared from the foundation of the world to be our Savior and Redeemer, that the accounts of his life are true. To believe on Christ is to know that Jesus had within him power that no other mortal man had—the power to lay down his life and take it again—and that he can forgive our sins and raise us from the grave. To believe on Christ is to have the inward assurance that he can renew our souls and make us men and women of purpose. To believe on Christ is to do the works he would do if he were ministering on earth, for true faith is always manifest in faithfulness.

Simon Peter answered him, Lord, to whom shall we go? thou
hast the words of eternal life. And we believe and are sure
that thou art that Christ, the Son of the living God.
—JOHN 6:68–69

Christ is the Way, indeed, the only way back to God.
He is the Truth, the real truth. He is the Life, our only
hope for deliverance from death and sorrow and endless torment. To wander from him is to stray from
peace and happiness. To choose an alternate source of
salvation is to make a foolish and short-sighted decision, to choose emptiness and anguish of soul. Truly,
those who have acquired a witness of the Master's
divine Sonship, received a remission of sins through
the power of his atoning blood, and enjoyed the sweet
fruits of the Spirit in daily living cannot in good conscience turn back to their old life, cannot settle for
second best, cannot find peace or satisfaction in any
other enterprise, no matter how noble. Once we have
chosen Christ, there is only Christ.

For out of the heart proceed evil thoughts, murders, adulteries,
fornications, thefts, false witness, blasphemies:
these are the things which defile a man:
but to eat with unwashen hands defileth not a man.
—MATTHEW 15:19–20

Though they are important, clean hands are far less important than clean hearts. When our hearts are free of envy, malice, and wickedness, our actions are righteous, and we are filled with love. In the early days of the restored Church, the Lord said he loved Hyrum Smith for the "integrity of his heart" (D&C 124:15). Hyrum's thoughts and actions were congruent, and so his words were edifying, good, and true. How often do we regret a thoughtless comment, a slip of the tongue, and resolve to watch ourselves more closely? Perhaps the better focus is not on restraint but on allowing the Lord to cleanse our hearts and purify our thoughts.

And from thence he arose, and went into the borders of
Tyre and Sidon, and entered into an house, and would
have no man know it: but he could not be hid.
—MARK 7:24

The Lord was weary, in need of respite. He sought solitude at times during his earthly ministry in order to be close to his Eternal Father and enter into that rest that comes only through communion with the Infinite. The account in Mark 7:24 in the King James Version may be puzzling to us at first, for it indicates that "he could not be hid." Certainly the Savior could be alone if he desired; he is the Lord of life, the God of the universe, and he has all power. But the Joseph Smith Translation clarifies the meaning of this passage: The Master "entered into a house, and would that no man should come unto him. But he could not deny them; for he had compassion upon all men" (JST Mark 7:22–23). Jesus' compassion and love for his brothers and sisters directs his eternal accessibility. It is clear that he was ever willing to be inconvenienced.

The Pharisees also with the Sadducees . . . desired him that he would shew them a sign from heaven. He answered, . . . O ye hypocrites, ye can discern the face of the sky; but can ye not discern the signs of the times?
—MATTHEW 16:1–3

Ironically, the canon of scripture was open for rabbinic interpretation but closed to him who came as the fulfillment of the Old Testament. "Ye know not Moses, neither the prophets," the Master declared, "for if ye had known them, ye would have believed on me; for to this intent they were written. For I am sent that ye might have life" (JST Luke 14:36). The Lord contrasted his enemies' ability to read the face of the sky, and thus discern signs associated with weather patterns, with their marked inability to read the signs of the times, and thus discern the true meanings of messianic prophecies and testimonies. How common it is for those equipped with this world's credentials to ignore the weak and the simple who have been called by the Almighty. One day the God of heaven will say to them, as did Alma to Korihor, "Thou hast had signs enough" (Alma 30:44).

A wicked and adulterous generation seeketh after a sign;
and there shall no sign be given unto it,
but the sign of the prophet Jonas.
—MATTHEW 16:4

Twice when he was asked for a sign from heaven, Jesus referred to Jonah, whose life story contained events that foreshadowed Jesus' own death, burial, and resurrection (Matthew 12:39–41; 16:4; Luke 11:29–30). Jesus directed his listeners' attention to his own great atoning sacrifice, the culmination of all prophetic signs and symbols, while condemning sign seeking. The Lord offers us signs of his coming so we will be vigilant and prepared. But we are not to be consumed with watching and waiting, speculating and prognosticating. Those who seek for signs, as did Sherem and Korihor, manifest pride and spiritual weakness. We are warned against looking for signs to consume upon our lusts (D&C 46:9). Signs come by the will of God and not of man (D&C 63:10). Most often, signs come after the trial of our faith and follow those who believe (Ether 12:6; D&C 63:9–11; 84:65–72).

Jesus . . . asked his disciples, saying, Whom do men say that I the Son of man am? And they said, Some say that thou art John the Baptist: some, Elias; and others, Jeremias, or one of the prophets.
—MATTHEW 16:13–14

Who do men say that I the Son of God am?" asked Jesus. That is the question of the ages. Everything both here and hereafter depends on how we answer this question and what we do with our answer. Some speculated that Jesus was John the Baptist raised from the dead or a metaphysical embodiment of someone who would perform a mighty work and prepare the way for the return of the Messiah. But Jesus Christ is none of these. He is more than a prophet, more than a teacher of truth or a preacher of righteousness. He is much more than a master educator, a kindly philosopher, or a traveling messenger of good will. He is who he says he is: the Son of God, the Only Begotten of the Father, our Redeemer, Lord, and King.

MAY

*Suffer the little children to come
unto me, and forbid them not: for
of such is the kingdom of God.*

—MARK 10:14

But whom say ye that I am? And Simon Peter answered and said,
Thou art the Christ, the Son of the living God.
—MATTHEW 16:15–16

Our thoughts, words, and actions are perhaps the best summary of who we say Jesus is. Especially worthy of examination are the testimonies of those who, like the apostle Peter, have been called as special witnesses of Christ. President Gordon B. Hinckley has said: "Jesus Christ is the Son of God, who condescended to come into this world of misery, struggle and pain, to touch men's hearts for good, to teach the way of eternal life, and to give Himself as a sacrifice for the sins of all mankind. . . . How much truer, how much deeper is our love and appreciation and respect one for another because of Him. How infinite is our opportunity for exaltation made possible through His redeeming love" (*Teachings of Gordon B. Hinckley,* 286). Such a testimony of the Master is not reserved for prophets and apostles; it comes as a gift of the Spirit to those who seek (D&C 46:13). All can know.

And Jesus answered and said unto him, Blessed art thou, Simon
Bar-jona: for flesh and blood hath not revealed it unto thee,
but my Father which is in heaven. And I say also unto thee,
That thou art Peter, and upon this rock I will build my
church; and the gates of hell shall not prevail against it.
—MATTHEW 16:17–18

Peter's witness of Jesus Christ came to him, as such a witness comes to all of us, by direct revelation from God through the power of the Holy Ghost. The work of the Lord in any age is founded upon both institutional and individual revelation. The Prophet Joseph taught: "Jesus in His teaching says, 'Upon this rock I will build my Church, and the gates of hell shall not prevail against it.' What rock? Revelation" (*Teachings of the Prophet Joseph Smith,* 274). As long as men and women prove worthy of personal revelation and sustain and uphold the apostles and prophets charged to receive divine direction for the Lord's kingdom, the gates of hell—the power and dominion of the devil— cannot prevail against the earthly Church.

I will give unto thee the keys of the kingdom of heaven:
and whatsoever thou shalt bind on earth shall be
bound in heaven: and whatsoever thou shalt
loose on earth shall be loosed in heaven.
—MATTHEW 16:19

Jesus came to earth as the Savior and Redeemer of all humankind. He came to suffer and bleed and die for our sins, to rise from the dead, to teach us the only way to happiness here and hereafter. And as the great High Priest, he came as a legal administrator to organize his church, bestow the keys of the kingdom of God, confer the higher priesthood, and ordain men to offices within that priesthood. "In all ages of the world, whenever the Lord has given a dispensation of the priesthood to any man by actual revelation, or any set of men, this power has always been given. Hence, whatsoever those men did in authority, in the name of the Lord, and did it truly and faithfully, . . . it became a law on earth and in heaven, and could not be annulled, according to the decrees of the great Jehovah" (D&C 128:9).

And whosoever will lose his life in this world, for my sake,
shall find it in the world to come. Therefore, forsake the world,
and save your souls; for what is a man profited,
if he shall gain the whole world, and lose his own soul?
—JST Matthew 16:28- 29

The paradox of losing our lives for Jesus' sake in order to save them gives vital perspective to all who seek to follow Christ. When he invites us to take up our cross, he teaches that all of us will have burdens to bear and personal crosses to carry (JST Matthew 16:26). How we choose to bear these burdens will make all the difference. If we decide to save our lives by refusing to submit our will to the Lord, real peace and joy will elude us—now and in the world to come. But if we humbly follow the Savior's example and willingly take up our cross, we activate the Atonement in our lives. We will be strengthened, carried in our carrying, and our souls will find rest.

After six days Jesus taketh Peter, James, and John his brother,
and bringeth them up into an high mountain apart, and was
transfigured before them. . . . And behold, there appeared
unto them Moses and Elias talking with him.
—MATTHEW 17:1–3

One week after Simon Peter's confession and statement of testimony, some six months before the atonement and death of our Lord, Jesus took his meridian
First Presidency onto the mountain to pray. The four
were transfigured, lifted spiritually to a higher plane,
to behold sacred and profound things. They saw a
vision of the ultimate transfiguration of the earth
(D&C 63:20–21) and, in fulfillment of the Savior's
word just one week earlier, received the keys of the
kingdom of God. Using as our pattern a similar event
in the Kirtland Temple on 3 April 1836 (D&C 110),
we suppose that Moses conferred the keys of the gathering of Israel, Elias conferred the keys associated with
celestial marriage and the patriarchal order, and Elijah
conferred the sacred sealing powers necessary to bind
and seal families forever. The Twelve were thereby
empowered to lead the Church of Christ.

Jesus said unto him, If thou canst believe,
all things are possible to him that believeth. And straightway
the father of the child cried out, and said with tears,
Lord, I believe; help thou mine unbelief.
—MARK 9:23–24

A father brings his son to Jesus to be healed. Like all good fathers, he wants his son to be made whole, but he is well aware of his child's infirmities. As much as he wants to believe, he knows his faith needs to be stronger. He receives the Savior's affirmation and acts upon his particle of faith, pleading now that the Master will not only heal his child but also strengthen his faith. The boy is healed, and perhaps just as remarkably, the belief of the father is strengthened. Both healings are miracles. In keeping with scriptural injunction, the father did not receive the blessing until after the trial of his faith (Ether 12:6). Nothing is withheld from those who abide the law of faith which qualifies them to receive it (D&C 82:10). Nothing is impossible for the Lord—or for those who believe.

And when he was come into the house, his disciples asked him privately, Why could not we cast him out? And he said unto them, This kind can come forth by nothing, but by prayer and fasting.
—MARK 9:28–29

Some tasks require of us a deeper spirituality, a heightened awareness of victory over self and of communion with the Infinite than do others (McKay, *Gospel Ideals,* 390). Some Goliaths in our lives require us to fast, to pray and plead with an unusual intensity, to supplicate the Almighty for his power and strength. The Lord inquired of his prophet Isaiah, "Is not this the fast that I have chosen? to loose the bands of wickedness, to undo the heavy burdens, and to let the oppressed go free, and that ye break every yoke?" (Isaiah 58:6). Fasting brings power. Fasting, in combination with sincere and earnest prayer, brings strength beyond our own.

Verily I say unto you, Except ye be converted, and become as little children, ye shall not enter into the kingdom of heaven. Whosoever therefore shall humble himself as this little child, the same is greatest in the kingdom of heaven.

— MATTHEW 18:3–4

The apostle Paul taught, "Brethren, be not children in understanding: howbeit in malice be ye children, but in understanding be men" (1 Corinthians 14:20). We are to be wise, yet harmless (Matthew 10:16); bold, yet not overbearing (Alma 38:12); unashamed of declaring the gospel, yet meek and lowly of heart (Romans 1:16; Moroni 7: 44). King Benjamin outlines the qualities of those who yield to the enticings of the Holy Spirit, put off the natural man, and become Saints through the atonement of Christ. They become as children: submissive, meek, humble, patient, full of love, and willing to submit to all things which the Lord sees fit to inflict upon them (Mosiah 3:19). True greatness is largely a measure of our hearts. It comes not by honors received, callings held, or wealth and status achieved. Greatness in the kingdom of heaven comes from developing the attributes of godliness and becoming as a little child.

*And whosoever shall offend one of these little ones that believe in
me, it is better for him that a millstone were hanged
about his neck, and he were cast into the sea.*
—MARK 9:42

To be drowned in the depths of the ocean would be better than to receive the punishment affixed to abusing a child. Such maltreatment or neglect is condemned by the Lord and his prophets in the strongest terms—and always has been. The prophetic warnings in "The Family: A Proclamation to the World" are clear: "Parents have a sacred duty to rear their children in love and righteousness, to provide for their physical and spiritual needs. . . . Mothers and fathers will be held accountable before God for the discharge of these obligations" (*Ensign,* November 1995, 102). We have a responsibility to nurture and love other family members and to foster their eternal growth and happiness. The Lord has commanded that we "become as little children" in order to enter his kingdom (Matthew 18:3). Rather than forcing our ways onto them, we are admonished to conform our ways to theirs—to be more humble, teachable, submissive, and loving.

Woe unto the world because of offences!
For it must needs be that offences come;
but woe to that man by whom the offence cometh!
—MATTHEW 18:7

Lehi taught that opposition is necessary in all things. "If not so, . . . righteousness could not be brought to pass, neither wickedness, neither holiness nor misery, neither good nor bad" (2 Nephi 2:11). If temptation and sin were not within reach, then strength of character here and eternal glory hereafter could not be achieved. At the same time, though opposition is part of the plan, there is no need to volunteer for them. We do not build monuments to Judas Iscariot, praise the leaders of the Jews, or compliment the Roman soldiers for their part in delivering the Son of God to the cross, even though that cross brings salvation. Satan does not need our help to do his job, nor does the Lord need us to misbehave so that others might overcome. As Jesus said in the Sermon on the Mount, "Sufficient unto the day shall be the evil thereof" (JST Matthew 6:39).

If a man have an hundred sheep, and one of them be gone astray,
doth he not leave the ninety and nine . . . and seeketh that
which is gone astray? And if it so be that he find it,
verily I say unto you, he rejoiceth more of that sheep,
than of the ninety and nine which went not astray.
—MATTHEW 18:12–13

The parable of the lost sheep illustrates the depth of the Savior's love for us as well as our inherent worth as sons and daughters of God. The Lord declared, "I am the good shepherd and know my sheep. . . . I lay down my life for the sheep" (John 10:14–15). He knows us individually, knows our individual needs, and gives us individual love and attention. Nonetheless, like the prodigal son, we lose our way from time to time. We may not move to a far country and take up riotous living, but we do sometimes lose sight of who and Whose we really are (Luke 15:11–32). Yet the Good Shepherd's concern for us is constant. "The good shepherd doth call after you; and if you will hearken unto his voice he will bring you into his fold, and ye are his sheep" (Alma 5:60).

If thy brother shall trespass against thee, go and tell him his fault
between thee and him alone: if he shall hear thee,
thou hast gained thy brother.
—MATTHEW 18:15

We are to be courageously proactive and kind-heartedly private about clearing up offenses in our relationships with others. We can extend an olive branch and be true brothers and sisters in our families, the Church, and our communities. "Let every man esteem his brother as himself," the Lord said in our day. "I say unto you, be one; and if ye are not one ye are not mine" (D&C 38:24, 27). Elder Bruce R. McConkie reminds us: "The Lord commands the innocent person, the one without fault, the one who has been offended, to search out his brother and seek to repair the breach. Thus: If thy brother trespass against thee, wait not for him to repent and make restitution; he is already somewhat hardened in spirit because of the trespass itself; rather, go to him, extend the hand of fellowship, shower him with love, and per-chance 'thou hast gained thy brother'" (*Doctrinal New Testament Commentary,* 1:422–23).

For where two or three are gathered together in my name,
there am I in the midst of them.
—MATTHEW 18:20

The Almighty works with nations and kingdoms and directs the destiny of multitudes of people. But enlightenment and conversion take place with individuals, in the heart and mind of this man and that woman, in the soul of this boy and that girl. There is no requirement that a large group must be met together for the spirit of revelation to be manifest, no limit of numbers of people below which God's power cannot be felt. Thus in the smallest branch in the most remote area of the world, Saints of God may be lifted by singing the songs of Zion and edified by hearing the word of truth proclaimed by the power of the Holy Ghost. And, thankfully, even while all alone, each of us may enjoy the sweet companionship of the Lord through the quiet, peaceful outpouring of his Spirit. Truly, our Savior ministers to us one by one.

Then came Peter to him, and said, Lord, how oft shall my
brother sin against me, and I forgive him? till seven times?
Jesus saith unto him, I say not unto thee,
Until seven times: but, Until seventy times seven.
—MATTHEW 18:21–22

We know how hard the practice of forgiveness can be. It can be very hard, even soul-wrenching. President Gordon B. Hinckley observed: "We are all prone to brood on the evil done us. That brooding becomes as a gnawing and destructive canker. Is there a virtue more in need of application in our time than the virtue of forgiving and forgetting? . . . There is no peace in the nursing of a grudge. There is no happiness in living for the day when you can 'get even'" (*Teachings of Gordon B. Hinckley,* 228). Withholding forgiveness has been compared to eating poison and waiting for the other person to die. No matter how deep the hurt, how sensitive the sore spot, we can find strength to forgive when we draw upon the healing and enabling power of Jesus Christ. When we remember our own need for forgiveness, we open our hearts in love to others.

Now the Jews' feast of tabernacles was at hand. His brethren
therefore said unto him, Depart hence, and go into Judaea,
that thy disciples also may see the works that thou doest.
. . . For neither did his brethren believe in him.
—JOHN 7:2–5

There is loneliness in knowing the truth and having
those closest to us—friends or family members—fail
to understand what we know or appreciate what we
do. When Jesus' "friends heard him speak, they went
out to lay hold on him; for they said, He is beside himself" (JST Mark 3:16). Some of the children of Mary
and Joseph, brought up in the same home with Jesus,
refused at first to accept the divine Sonship of their
older brother. It must have been difficult for Jesus to
sense their resistance, witness their unbelief, and
respond lovingly to their ridicule. Truly and ironically,
Jesus taught that "a man's foes shall be they of his own
household" (Matthew 10:36). It is comforting to know
that some, if not all, of the Lord's brothers did accept
the faith and participate in the ministry, one of them
becoming an apostle and the author of a New Testament epistle.

They said, Lord, wilt thou that we command fire to come down from heaven, and consume them, even as Elias did? But he turned, and rebuked them, and said, Ye know not what manner of spirit ye are of. For the Son of man is not come to destroy men's lives, but to save them.

—LUKE 9:54–56

James and John, the "sons of thunder" (Mark 3:17), zealously suggested severe punishment for those who rejected the Master. But then, as today, the Savior instructs otherwise. He teaches that it is wrong to force compliance or flaunt power. The more powerful message is always the gospel of peace and salvation. The sure knowledge that Jesus is the Christ is better conveyed by turning the other cheek. As the Lord demonstrates, the true spirit of the gospel is good news, not gloom; charity, not hatred; blessings, not cursings; salvation, not damnation; life, not death. "For God sent not his Son into the world to condemn the world; but that the world through him might be saved" (John 3:17). Christ is come to bring eternal life and everlasting joy to those who partake of his goodness, receive of his grace, and enter into covenant with him. This is his pure love, which endures forever (Moroni 7:47).

A certain man said unto him, Lord, I will follow thee
whithersoever thou goest. And Jesus said unto him,
Foxes have holes, and birds of the air have nests; but
the Son of man hath not where to lay his head.
—LUKE 9:57–58

How ironic that the Savior of the world, he who would make it possible for all mankind to return to their heavenly home, was not a householder during his mortal ministry. He taught and traveled without purse or scrip. Yet, in another sense, he owned everything. Under the Father's direction, he was the creator of this and other worlds. The wind and the waves would obey his will. He was the Mighty One (Isaiah 60:16), the King of the earth and Lord of all (Acts 10:36), the Author and Finisher of our faith (Hebrews 12:2). Those who wholeheartedly respond to his message and embrace him are willing to follow him and do all that he asks of them, including sacrifice this world's toys and trappings. They understand that submission to divine will is the key to freedom. Obedience opens the door to ultimate victory and never-ending joy in our heavenly home.

And [Jesus] said unto another, Follow me. But he said,
Lord, suffer me first to go and bury my father.
Jesus said unto him, Let the dead bury their dead:
but go thou and preach the kingdom of God.
—LUKE 9:59–60

No one loves us with deeper or more tender regard than does our Lord and Savior, and surely no one knows the pain associated with the loss of a loved one better than he. By saying "Let the dead bury their dead," Jesus was not suggesting that people, even the people of the covenant, should not mourn for the loss of those who die. Rather, he was emphasizing the need for stable and steady discipleship, for continuing in his word and remaining at our duty station. Mormon pleaded with Moroni, "We have a labor to perform whilst in this tabernacle of clay, that we may conquer the enemy of all righteousness, and rest our souls in the kingdom of God" (Moroni 9:6). While we must attend appropriately to those matters of life and death that are ever a part of this mortal experience, we must not be preoccupied with them; we have an eternal labor to perform.

*Another also said, Lord, I will follow thee; but let me first go bid
them farewell, which are at home at my house. And Jesus
said unto him, No man, having put his hand to the plough,
and looking back, is fit for the kingdom of God.*
—LUKE 9:61–62

Bidding farewell to loved ones at home seems worthy enough, but once we have put our hand to the plough, once we have covenanted to follow the Master, we must begin the work. If we keep one foot on gospel soil and one in the world, glance back longingly, or vacillate with disheartening doubt and fear, we cannot expect to reap the blessings of discipleship. Inspirational stories abound of innumerable faithful Saints embracing the gospel without looking back, abandoning habits and false ideas, and leaving country, family, traditions, and cultures to build the kingdom of God. They hearken to the voice of the Spirit, heed the call to ascend to higher ground, and follow a living prophet. With conviction, they "forsake the world" (D&C 53:2), lose an old way of living, and find a new and immensely more fulfilling one.

Jesus answered them, and said, My doctrine is not mine,
but his that sent me. If any man will do his will,
he shall know of the doctrine, whether it be of God,
or whether I speak of myself.
—JOHN 7:16–17

The experiment of faith begins with planting the seed. The seeker after truth allows the seed to swell within his soul for a season, prays about it, and performs works of righteousness and service. Then comes the assurance that Jesus is indeed the Christ, the Divine Redeemer. Hope is followed by action, which leads to a confirmation. In short, we receive a witness after the trial of our faith (Ether 12:6). We come to know that tithing is a divine law of economics by living the law of tithing. We come to know that the Word of Wisdom is a commandment from God by observing it. And we gain the assurance that The Church of Jesus Christ of Latter-day Saints is the kingdom of God on earth by completely immersing ourselves in the doctrines, practices, and programs of the Church. We do, and then we know.

If any man thirst, let him come unto me, and drink.
He that believeth on me, as the scripture hath said,
out of his belly shall flow rivers of living water.
—JOHN 7:33–38

Faith in Christ entails an acceptance of his gospel and submission to the principles and ordinances of that gospel. Thereafter, an ongoing and ever-growing belief in the Savior, the Fountain of Living Water, results in outpourings of his Spirit to comfort, teach, testify, and sanctify. Faith in Christ and complete surrender to him make us vessels of his righteousness, inspired instruments through which his light and truth and love are conveyed to the children of God. In our day, the Lord has said, "Unto him that keepeth my commandments I will give the mysteries of my kingdom, and the same shall be in him a well of living water, springing up unto everlasting life" (D&C 63:23).

Then came the officers to the chief priests and Pharisees;
and they said unto them, Why have ye not brought him?
The officers answered, Never man spake like this man.
Then answered them the Pharisees, Are ye also deceived?
—JOHN 7:45–47

C. S. Lewis wrote: "I am trying here to prevent any-one saying the really foolish thing that people often say about [Christ]: 'I'm ready to accept Jesus as a great moral teacher, but I don't accept His claim to be God.' That is the one thing we must not say. A man who was merely a man and said the sort of things Jesus said would not be a great moral teacher. He would either be a lunatic—on a level with the man who says he is a poached egg—or else he would be the Devil of Hell. You must make your choice. Either this man was, and is, the Son of God: or else a madman or something worse. . . . But let us not come with any patronizing nonsense about His being a great human teacher. He has not left that open to us. He did not intend to" (*Mere Christianity*, 45). Jesus was no ordinary man. He is the incomparable Christ.

*And the scribes and Pharisees brought unto him a woman taken
in adultery. . . . So when they continued asking him,
he lifted up himself, and said unto them, He that is
without sin among you, let him first cast a stone at her.*
—JOHN 8:3–7

Moses had declared adultery to be a capital crime, one for which both offenders were worthy of death. But where was the woman's partner in sin? The law of Moses also prescribed that the witnesses of the crime should initiate the execution. But only those not guilty of the same crime could take part. Thus the Master Teacher's words went into the accusers' hearts like a spear, and their retreat from the scene signaled their own guilt. How very often do people rush forward to confess the sins of others! Because none of us sees the whole picture, none of us knows enough to condemn another or attribute motives. Final judgment rests with the Omniscient One. The good news of the gospel is that we can change, that we can pick ourselves up, dust ourselves off, and, through the cleansing power of the blood of a sinless Savior, start anew.

Then spake Jesus again unto them, saying, I am the light of the world: he that followeth me shall not walk in darkness, but shall have the light of life.
—JOHN 8:12

With Jesus as our light, we have a sense of purpose and direction. We do not fear. We find comfort and peace, and we are able to make right choices. With his light, we truly see both who he is and who we are. In the dark, it is difficult to discern our path. Without the Light, we become lost, disoriented, and fearful. The psalmist declared, "The Lord is my light and my salvation; whom shall I fear?" (Psalm 27:1). In days of darkness and trouble, it is comforting to know that light is available. Jesus Christ can be our light and lead us into life eternal. His light illuminates our lives with hope and chases away the thick darkness of sin and death. The Light of the world gives us life.

*And he that sent me is with me: the Father hath not left me alone;
for I do always those things that please him.*
—JOHN 8:29

Jesus never took a backward step. He never took a moral detour. He never allowed his soul to be tainted by feelings of greed or jealousy or lust. He "was in all points tempted like as we are, yet without sin" (Hebrews 4:15). Consequently, he never forfeited the influence of his Father's Spirit. Theirs was a total communion, a divine oneness that attests both to our Lord's identity as the Son of God as well as to his complete fidelity to his Father. He knew what it was like to be rejected and scorned by men, to be excluded by myopic mortals, but all of that was tolerable because of his total oneness with the Father. Jesus' full consecration of soul enabled him to enjoy a fulness of the Spirit in mortality and prepared him to receive the fulness of the glory of the Father in the resurrection (JST John 3:34; D&C 93:16–17).

Then said Jesus to those Jews which believed on him,
If ye continue in my word, then are ye my disciples indeed;
and ye shall know the truth, and the truth shall make you free.
—JOHN 8:31–32

Christ is the Spirit of Truth and the Light of Truth. In him is no deception, no falsehood, no untruth. He knows all truth, lives all truth, and is all truth. As we embrace truth, we come unto him. We may know many things, but we will not know the Truth if we never embrace "the way, the truth, and the life" (John 14:6). Without the life and teachings of the Savior as our model for living truthfully, without the scriptures and living prophets as teachers of truth, without personal revelation that brings us to truth and empowers us to live truthfully, we are left to wander in error and darkness. Drawing closer to the Truth liberates us from the bondage of lust and addiction, frees us from the shackles of sin and false belief, and enables us to go forward with unlimited freedom into celestial life.

Jesus answered them, Verily, verily, I say unto you,
Whosoever committeth sin is the servant of sin.
—JOHN 8:34

Whenever we sow an evil action, we reap an unworthy habit. If not repented of, eventually those actions and habits result in a tarnished and tainted character. The apostle Paul wrote that "to whom ye yield yourselves servants to obey, his servants ye are to whom ye obey" (Romans 6:16). Peter noted that "of whom a man is overcome, of the same is he brought in bondage" (2 Peter 2:19). Simply put, service to Satan leads to slavery, for "the wages of sin is death" (Romans 6:23). On the other hand, obedience and surrender to Christ results in freedom, dynamic spontaneity, and mature individualism. "Being then made free from sin, [we become] the servants of righteousness" (Romans 6:18).

Verily, verily, I say unto you, If a man keep my saying,
he shall never see death.
—JOHN 8:51

Through Christ Jesus we are spiritually reborn and enjoy fulness of life. He brings salvation and never-ending life to those who believe and follow him. Our Savior taught, "He that heareth my word, and believeth on him that sent me, hath everlasting life . . . [and] is passed from death unto life" (John 5:24). He promised further, "Whosoever liveth and believeth in me shall never die" (John 11:26). In this dispensation, the Lord told the Prophet Joseph Smith, "Blessed are the dead that die in the Lord, from henceforth, when the Lord shall come, and old things shall pass away, and all things become new, they shall rise from the dead and shall not die after" (D&C 63:49). The Lord's work and glory is "to bring to pass the immortality and eternal life of man" (Moses 1:39). He promises ever-lasting life to all who will hear the words of God and do them.

Jesus said unto them, Verily, verily,
I say unto you, Before Abraham was, I am.
—JOHN 8:58

Abraham, the Father of the Faithful, was one of the great heroes of the Jews. Therefore, when Jesus taught that "if a man keep my saying, he shall never see death" (John 8:51), the Jewish leaders were infuriated. They promptly reminded the Master that Father Abraham had long since died, as had the other Old Testament prophets. To put things into perspective, therefore, Jesus testified, "Before Abraham was, I am." The words "I am" are related to the Hebrew name of God, Yahweh, or, as we know it, Jehovah. The Man from Nazareth thus offended the Jews both in speaking the unspeakable name of Deity and in identifying himself as that very Being. In essence, he said to them, "Before Abraham was I, Jehovah." Jesus knew who he was: he was God, the God of the ancients. He now bore that powerful testimony to those who had refused to accept his witness.

*Jesus said, For judgment I am come into this world,
that they which see not might see;
and that they which see might be made blind.*
—JOHN 9:39

Our Master is able to make us strong—each one of us—but only if we are willing to confess and acknowledge our weakness and thus our need for him. We are able to see only as the Lord peels away from our eyes the layers of sin and duplicity and self-assurance. Through Moroni, the Lord explained: "If men come unto me I will show unto them their weakness. I give unto men weakness that they may be humble; and my grace is sufficient for all men that humble themselves before me; for if they humble themselves before me, and have faith in me, then will I make weak things become strong unto them" (Ether 12:27; 2 Corinthians 12:9). Acknowledgment of our weakness, or mortal limitations, is the first step toward receiving divine strength and power.

I am come that they might have life,
and that they might have it more abundantly.

—JOHN 10:10

We hear much about how to *cope* with life. We cope with problems. We cope with unmerciful schedules. We cope with family challenges. Coping implies somehow getting through the present crisis, surviving the moment. Yet the Savior promises deliverance, liberation, and lasting peace. His solution is not simply to generate and maintain the power of positive thinking. He does not ask us to live in a world of denial. What he does ask is that we do our very best and then shift our remaining burdens to him, trust him, rely upon him. Jesus offers the abundant life—a life of perspective, a life of purpose, a life of maturity, a life of meaning. The abundant life is not free of troubles, not void of ironies and struggles, but it is filled with the peace and sweet assurance that God loves us and that he will be with us to the end.

JUNE

And Jesus said unto them, Come
ye after me, and I will make you
to become fishers of men.
—MARK 1:17

And other sheep I have, which are not of this fold:
them also I must bring, and they shall hear my voice;
and there shall be one fold, and one shepherd.
—JOHN 10:16

Christ is the Lord and Savior of all creation, and his ministry is to all nations, kindreds, tongues, and peoples. He loves the people of the western hemisphere as much as he loves the people of the eastern hemisphere and is as eager to save men and women in the Ukraine as in Chile. He orchestrates the events of this life to bring the gospel to as many of God's children as possible as soon as it is appropriate. "Know ye not that there are more nations than one?" he asked his servant Nephi. "Know ye not that I, the Lord your God, have created all men, and that I remember those who are upon the isles of the sea; and that I rule in the heavens above and in the earth beneath; and I bring forth my word unto the children of men, yea, even upon all the nations of the earth?" (2 Nephi 29:7).

Therefore doth my Father love me, because I lay down my life,
   that I might take it again. No man taketh it from me, . . .
I have power to lay it down, and I have power to take it again.
—JOHN 10:17–18

Jesus voluntarily surrendered his life, permitting his own death through an act of will. Born of Mary, a mortal mother, he inherited the capacity to die. Begotten by God, an immortal Father, he possessed the power to live forever. He could not die except by allowing himself to do so. No other "mortal" was thus qualified to be our Redeemer. In the Book of Mormon, Lehi explained this gospel truth, stating that the Messiah "layeth down his life according to the flesh, and taketh it again by the power of the Spirit, that he may bring to pass the resurrection of the dead, being the first that should rise" (2 Nephi 2:8). Jesus gave up his life because of his love for his Father and for us and because of his perfect submission to the Father's will.

Which now of these three, thinkest thou, was neighbour
unto him that fell among the thieves? And he said,
He that shewed mercy on him. Then said Jesus
unto him, Go, and do thou likewise.
—LUKE 10:36–37

In the parable of the good Samaritan, Jesus teaches us that we are all neighbors and that we all need mercy—the blessing of divine benevolence and human goodwill. Each of us wants mercy, and certainly all of us need it. How willing are we to show mercy to others? Do we favor stern justice? Or do we tenderly remember when we have cried, "Have mercy upon me, O Lord, for I am in trouble"? (Psalm 31:9). Mercy brings heaven and earth together in the most poignant way. The Lord, in his abundant mercy, blesses those who are merciful (Matthew 5:7). And though we cannot repay his divine grace, we can be the hands and hearts that reach out to others—down the block or around the world. We do well to remember, "The Lord is good; his mercy is everlasting" (Psalm 100:5).

JUNE 4

*Jesus answered and said unto her, Martha, Martha,
thou art careful and troubled about many things:
But one thing is needful: and Mary hath chosen that good part,
which shall not be taken away from her.*

—Luke 10:41–42

Martha was a devoted disciple of the Lord Jesus
Christ who "was not a whit behind" her sister in faithfulness and dedication (Helaman 11:19). On this
occasion, however, she was "cumbered about much
serving" (Luke 10:40)—burdened, worried, distracted
from learning because of where she had chosen to
expend her effort. The story of Mary and Martha is
about priorities, about where we place our emphasis
and direct our attention. It is so easy in our hectic
world to be ensnared by the peripherals and lose sight
of what matters most. Truly, the word of God is more
powerful than anything else in creating and nurturing
faith within our hearts. To the extent that we choose
the good part—that part which will not be taken from
us—we find the abundant life here and prepare ourselves for eternal life hereafter.

Woe unto you, lawyers! For ye have taken away the key
of knowledge, the fulness of the scriptures; ye enter
not in yourselves into the kingdom; and those
who were entering in, ye hindered.
—JST LUKE 11:53

Satan hates scripture. For centuries he kept the Bible from the children of men, and he does everything he can to create suspicion about the Book of Mormon and the scriptures of the Restoration. The father of lies motivates malicious mortals to remove plain and precious truths from holy writ by tampering with the text and corrupting simple meaning to "blind the eyes and harden the hearts of the children of men" (1 Nephi 13:27). Latter-day Saints rejoice in what God has revealed in the past, what he is now revealing through prophets and seers, and what things pertaining to the Lord's kingdom he shall yet make known. We cannot live a law or abide by a precept of which we are ignorant. The more of the revealed word we possess, the greater will be our tendency to search that word, incorporate it into our lives, and thereby come unto Christ.

*God said unto [the rich man], Thou fool, this night thy soul shall
be required of thee: then whose shall those things be,
which thou hast provided? So is he that layeth up
treasure for himself, and is not rich toward God.*
—LUKE 12:20–21

In the parable of the rich fool, the Lord teaches us
that those whose hearts are set on things of this world
will lose their reward hereafter. Earthly wealth has no
value in the heavenly realm, where treasures are incor-
ruptible and of inestimable worth. The story of Job in
the Old Testament teaches that anything earthly we
acquire—money, power, possessions, status—can be
lost, damaged, or stolen. But the riches of eternity—
the knowledge of truth, righteousness, gospel
covenants and ordinances, and family relationships—
will continue to be enjoyed and added upon in the
eternities. The foolishness of worldly preoccupation
with the treasures of earth leads inevitably to fear,
envy, and insecurity, but focusing on heavenly treasures brings peace, joy, and eternal reward.

*Be ye therefore ready also: for the Son of man
cometh at an hour when ye think not.*
—LUKE 12:40

A knowledge of what lies ahead can motivate individuals to greater devotion. The growing fascination in today's world with spiritual phenomena attests to the increasing yearning of men and women everywhere to know what lies ahead. As members of the Lord's Church, we take a wholesome and sane approach to prophecy. While we study and seek to understand the prophetic word, we strive to live each day with the conviction that God is in his heaven and will bring to pass his purposes in process of time. If we are prepared—if our lives are in order, if we are striving to keep our covenants—then we have neither an unhealthy obsession with the signs of the times nor an inordinate fear of what lies ahead. No matter what our mortal challenges may be or the uncertainty of the times, our minds are at peace. Our souls can rest.

Except ye repent, ye shall all likewise perish.
—LUKE 13:5

Adversity comes to all—good and bad, rich and poor, male and female. Suffering misfortune is no indicator of personal righteousness. We cannot assume that God is punishing us or sending retribution when we know that God's ways are higher than our ways, and his thoughts than our thoughts (Isaiah 55:9). We know of deeply spiritual individuals who have suffered mightily, whether with physical, economic, family, or other problems. But as they look to God for succor, they are refined and purified through the crucible of such experiences. They emerge with softened and contrite hearts. Although we do not comprehend the big picture at times, we know God preserves and protects his followers. He sends solace to aching souls. He comforts and reassures suffering mortals with his divine plan.

*Take my yoke upon you, and learn of me; for I am meek and
lowly in heart: and ye shall find rest unto your souls.
For my yoke is easy, and my burden is light.*
—MATTHEW 11:29–30

Christ invites us to come unto him and find rest to
our souls, to take his yoke upon us by learning of him,
walking his path, and abiding in him. We come unto
him by rejecting sin and accepting him as our Savior.
"If ye do this, he will, according to his own will and
pleasure, deliver you out of bondage" (Mosiah 7:33).
When we feel burdened by sin, sorrow, or regret, the
most difficult step can be realizing that we need a yoke
at all. The natural man would have us believe we can
solve our own problems. But life has a way of helping
us learn to submit humbly. Sooner or later we realize
that with the weight of the world on our shoulders,
the way to find rest to our souls is by yoking ourselves
to Christ. He will help us bear our burdens. He alone
brings lasting peace, happiness, and freedom.

I and my Father are one.
—JOHN 10:30

Latter-day Saints believe that the simplest reading of the New Testament text produces the simplest conclusion: The Father, the Son, and the Holy Ghost are three Gods, separate and distinct personages. They are one in purpose, one in mind, one in glory, one in divine attributes. We become one with the Father and the Son as we seek for and cultivate the Spirit in our lives. That is, we gain "the mind of Christ" (1 Corinthians 2:16) and come to think as the Master thinks, feel as he feels, and do as he does. "And the Father and I are one," the Savior declared in our day. "I am in the Father and the Father in me; and inasmuch as ye have received me, ye are in me and I in you" (D&C 50:43).

Jesus answered them, Is it not written in your law,
I said, Ye are gods?
—JOHN 10:34

Like Christ, we are made in the image of God (Genesis 1:27; Moses 2:27). Thus it is neither robbery nor heresy for the children of God to aspire to godhood (Matthew 5:48). Like any parent, our Heavenly Father wants his children to become all that he is. We become as God is through the atonement of Jesus Christ, through being transformed by the Spirit and cleansed of sins and sinfulness. We become as God is through learning to do, feel, think, say, and act as God would do, feel, think, say, and act. We will never oust God the Eternal Father or his Only Begotten Son, the Gods we worship. God, our Father in Heaven, has ordained a plan whereby, through the mediation of his Beloved Son, we might enjoy happiness in this world and dwell with him and be like him in the world to come.

JUNE 12

*Whosoever he be of you that forsaketh not all that he hath,
he cannot be my disciple.*
—LUKE 14:33

The Lord wants a whole-souled commitment from his disciples; he does not accept broken covenants or soon-to-be-forgotten promises. Throughout scripture, half-hearted Saints are condemned. If we live too much in the world, we will not receive the blessings promised to the faithful. Occasional bursts of faithfulness, even many good intentions, will not build a tower of true discipleship. Only a willingness to put the Lord first in everything will allow us to reach the kingdom of God. It may seem a high price to pay, but it is well worth the investment of time, talent, and all that we possess. In truth, it's a debt we owe to our Creator. King Benjamin taught: "If ye should serve [God] with all your whole souls yet ye would be unprofitable servants. And behold, all that he requires of you is to keep his commandments" (Mosiah 2:21–22).

Likewise, I say unto you, there is joy in the presence of the
angels of God over one sinner that repenteth.
—LUKE 15:10

In the parable of the lost coin, Jesus teaches us to watch over his children. He compares the joy of a woman who finds her lost coin to the rejoicing in the heavens when erring souls return to the path leading to eternal life. "Remember the worth of souls is great in the sight of God. . . . And how great is his joy in the soul that repenteth!" (D&C 18:10–13). Saints have a responsibility to seek for lost souls. We are to lift and bless one another, striving to avoid giving offense or leading someone astray. Our example of long-suffering kindness, faithfulness, and humility combined with patient concern can be the means for "finding" a lost soul. When people feel loved and accepted as fellow children of God, they are drawn from their hiding places to embrace gospel truths.

*But when he was yet a great way off, his father saw him, and had
compassion, and ran, and fell on his neck, and kissed him.*

—LUKE 15:20

In a sense, the parable of the prodigal son distils the
essence of Jesus' teachings. It is a story that might be
told of each of us, a tale of one who left a righteous
home and wandered into telestial territory. Such wan-
derers often come to themselves and realize what they
once had—not just three square meals a day but a
regular diet of love and patience and concern. Like so
many of the Master's teachings, this story may not
seem fair, at least from our limited perspective. But we
know that the eternal plan of the Father is a plan of
mercy. All of us are in desperate need of mercy, for we
are all sinners. Whether we stray out of ignorance,
neglect, or knowingly, God stands ready and willing to
receive us. "It was meet that we should make merry,
and be glad: for this thy brother was dead, and is alive
again; and was lost, and is found" (Luke 15:32).

*And the lord commended the unjust steward, because he had done
wisely. . . . And I say unto you, Make to yourselves friends
of the mammon of unrighteousness; that, when ye fail,
they may receive you into everlasting habitations.*
—LUKE 16:8–9

The parable of the unjust steward contrasts the care
that the "children of this world" take of their material
possessions with the sometimes careless attitude the
"children of light" have for that which is of lasting
worth (Luke 16:8). The Lord wants us not to adopt
the devotion to mammon of "the children of this
world" but rather to become full-hearted in our commitment to eternal things. Elder James E. Talmage
taught that we should "take a lesson from even the dishonest and the evil; if they are so prudent as to provide for the only future they think of, how much more
should you, who believe in an eternal future, provide
therefor! . . . Emulate the unjust steward and the lovers
of mammon, not in their dishonesty, cupidity, and
miserly hoarding of the wealth that is at best but tran-
sitory, but in their zeal, forethought, and provision for
the future" (*Jesus the Christ*, 464).

If they hear not Moses and the prophets,
neither will they be persuaded, though one rose from the dead.
—LUKE 16:31

Someone has wisely observed that when a man demands a sign, the last thing in the world he really wants is a sign. A person who spurns the quiet sign of the Spirit—the sign that comes to the soul through studying or hearing the word—is not likely to respond affirmatively to the loud janglings of physical evidence that present themselves to the outward senses. The things of God are known only by the power of the Spirit of God. They are to be comprehended not in the wind, the earthquake, or the fire, but through the workings of the still, small voice (1 Kings 19:11–12). Truly, "faith cometh not by signs, but signs follow those that believe" (D&C 63:9).

*And the Lord said, If ye had faith as a grain of mustard seed,
ye might say unto this sycamine tree, Be thou plucked up by the
root, and be thou planted in the sea; and it should obey you.*
—LUKE 17:6

The Savior uses the example of a mustard seed to explain how even the smallest desire for faith can grow. All prophets have taught the principle of faith. Paul said, "Faith is the substance of things hoped for, the evidence of things not seen" (Hebrews 11:1). Alma explained that to increase our faith, we must "experiment upon [his] words, and exercise a particle of faith" (Alma 32:27). If we want more faith in a principle of the gospel, we must be willing to live that principle more fully. Increased faith will follow our obedience. Moroni taught: "Ye receive no witness until after the trial of your faith. . . . For if there be no faith among the children of men God can do no miracle among them; wherefore, he showed not himself until after their faith" (Ether 12:6–12). The Lord will not manifest himself in our lives until we actively follow him and live his teachings.

Jesus said unto her, I am the resurrection, and the life: he that believeth in me, though he were dead, yet shall he live: And whosoever liveth and believeth in me shall never die.
—JOHN 11:25–26

In one clear and simple sentence, Jesus summarizes his life, his mission, and the entire gospel plan: He is the Resurrection—the first fruits of them who slept, the first to rise from the dead. He is Life. Through his atoning sacrifice, we can be forgiven, experience a mighty change of heart, and become new creatures in him (2 Corinthians 5:17; Mosiah 27:25–26). All who are dead, physically or spiritually, can be brought back into everlasting life only because of him. His atonement, death, and resurrection make immortality and eternal life possible for all humankind. Those who believe in him and strive to keep his commandments will never die in any ultimate sense (John 8:51). They are the valiant, the faithful, the believers whose lives declare unwaveringly: Thou art the Christ, the Son of the living God.

When Jesus therefore saw [Mary, the sister of Lazarus]
weeping, and the Jews also weeping, . . . he . . . was troubled,
and said, Where have ye laid [Lazarus]?
They said unto him, Lord, come and see. Jesus wept.
—JOHN 11:33–35

Life's starkest reality is death. It is one of the few
things every mortal shares without regard to earthly
status and accomplishments. And though the perspective given us by the gospel of Jesus Christ is help-
ful at the death of a loved one, it does not take away
the pain of loss. We may have an unshakable conviction of the immortality of the soul and of an eventual
reunion with loved ones, but still we grieve at their
temporary departure. He who knows us best, he who
is "touched with the feeling of our infirmities"
(Hebrews 4:15), knows fully the pain of such separation. "Thou shalt live together in love," he stated in
modern revelation, "insomuch that thou shalt weep
for the loss of them that die" (D&C 42:45). The only
way to take pain out of death is to take love out of life.

And when he thus had spoken, he cried with a loud voice,
Lazarus, come forth. And he that was dead came forth.
—JOHN 11:43–44

The poignant account of Jesus raising Lazarus from death "after [Lazarus] had lain in the grave four days already" (John 11:17) is powerful testimony that the Master is indeed the Resurrection and the Life. It is also a witness of the miraculous power of faith and love. Jesus loved Lazarus and his faithful sisters, Mary and Martha. He wanted to serve them. He knew this could be a great teaching moment, a never-to-be-forgotten testament of his divine Sonship. At least twice before, Jesus had raised the dead: the daughter of Jairus (Luke 8:41–42, 49–56) and the son of the widow of Nain (Luke 7:11–17). With these miracles, he not only raised the dead but instilled new spiritual life in the believers who witnessed them.

And Jesus answering said, Were there not ten [lepers]cleansed?
but where are the nine? There are not found that returned
to give glory to God, save this stranger.
—LUKE 17:17–18

How often do we redirect ourselves, even just our thoughts, to express gratitude? Only one of ten lepers came back to offer thanks. How often do we? Certainly, the Lord did not need their thanks; but the lepers needed the blessings that come from being thankful. Do we experience those blessings in our lives? Gratitude is a measure of our hearts. Giving thanks opens our hearts to others—and to God. A thankful heart is a companion to meekness and a close friend of forgiveness, peace, and love. Expressions of thanks direct our thoughts to God, the Fount of every blessing, and touch the cold realities of mortality with the warmth of heaven's light. In the whirlwind of daily living, gratitude invites holiness into our lives.

In that day, he which shall be upon the housetop, and his
stuff in the house, let him not come down to take it
away: and he that is in the field, let him likewise
not return back. Remember Lot's wife.
—LUKE 17:31–32

Once we have made the crucial decision to forsake the world and worldliness, then it is vital not to waste time or dissipate spiritual energy in contemplating what it would have been like to have stayed. Lot and his family were commanded to make a hasty exit from the wicked and perverse cities of Sodom and Gomorrah: "Escape for thy life; look not behind thee," Jehovah declared (Genesis 19:17). God "overthrew those cities, and all the plain, and all the inhabitants of the cities, and that which grew upon the ground. But [Lot's] wife looked back from behind him, and she became a pillar of salt" (Genesis 19:25–26). For one who has chosen to flee the grasp of Satan and enter the embrace of Jesus, the clarion call resounds: "Don't look back!"

The Pharisee stood and prayed thus with himself, God,
I thank thee that I am not as other men are. . . . And the
publican, standing afar off, . . . smote upon his breast,
saying, God be merciful to me a sinner.
—LUKE 18:10–13

The Pharisees considered themselves a step above other Jews in their observance of religious practices and ritual. Publicans collected taxes for the Roman government and were considered traitors to their nation. Frequently, they prospered by charging more than was fair and keeping the difference. In the story of the Pharisee and the publican, the Pharisee seems really not to need God; his impressive deeds are, he supposes, sufficient to save him. The publican, on the other hand, acknowledging his lowly station before man and God, simply pleads for mercy. A stark contrast, surely. But the sinful publican, not the pious Pharisee, goes home forgiven, for "he that humbleth himself shall be exalted" (Luke 18:14). All of us need mercy. Recognition of our spiritual bankruptcy without divine assistance is the beginning of wisdom, the door that opens us to strength beyond our own.

Then were there brought unto him little children,
that he should put his hands on them and pray.
And the disciples rebuked them, saying, There is no need,
for Jesus hath said, Such shall be saved.
—JST MATTHEW 19:13

The gospel restored in the latter-days has brought
back a plain and precious truth lost through long
centuries of misunderstanding: Little children are
saved through the atoning sacrifice of Jesus Christ
(Moroni 8; D&C 29:46–47; 93:38). Adam was taught:
"The Son of God hath atoned for original guilt,
wherein the sins of the parents cannot be answered
upon the heads of the children, for they are whole
from the foundation of the world" (Moses 6:54).
What comfort this sweet doctrine gives! Children who
die under the age of accountability will inherit eternal
glory. Mormon declared, "Teach parents that they
must repent and be baptized, and humble themselves
as their little children, and they shall all be saved with
their little children. And their little children need no
repentance, neither baptism. . . . [For] little children
are alive in Christ, even from the foundation of the
world" (Moroni 8:10–12).

Jesus said unto [the young man], If thou wilt be perfect,
go and sell that thou hast, and give to the poor,
and thou shalt have treasure in heaven:
and come and follow me.
—MATTHEW 19:21

A young man, a lawyer or scribe (Luke 10:25), asked the Savior which of all the commandments was the most important in qualifying for eternal life. Clearly, the answer to such a question is the commandment we are having the greatest difficulty living at the time. In this case, Jesus—who knew well the soul of this man— went straight to the heart of the matter, and the young man "went away sorrowful" (Luke 19:22). The Master perceived that the lawyer's trust in his riches was greater than his trust in God. Indeed, the man had become possessed by his possessions. It is difficult to lay hold on eternal life when our hands are grasping this world's goods.

It is easier for a camel to go through the eye of a needle,
than for a rich man to enter into the kingdom of God.
—MARK 10:25

Jesus said it is impossible to serve both God and mammon, and James, the brother of the Lord, wrote, "A double minded man is unstable in all his ways" (James 1:8). Only when we are willing to sacrifice all things—including our life, if necessary—can we come to know that our course is pleasing to God. Only then can we exercise the level of faith that leads to salvation. No metaphor was intended when Jesus spoke of camels and needles, for his disciples "were astonished out of measure, saying among themselves, Who then can be saved? And Jesus, looking upon them, said, With men that trust in riches, it is impossible; but not impossible with men who trust in God and leave all for my sake, for with such all these things are possible" (JST Mark 10:25–26).

There is no man that hath left house, or brethren, or sisters,
or father, or mother, or wife, or children, or lands, for my sake,
and the gospel's, But he shall receive an hundredfold . . .
and in the world to come eternal life.
—MARK 10:29–30

The Prophet Joseph taught, "A religion that does not require the sacrifice of all things never has power sufficient to produce the faith necessary [to lead] unto life and salvation" (*Lectures on Faith,* 6:7). All who forsake false beliefs, families, homes, and wealth in establishing Zion and sharing the gospel with others make sacrifices that will not be forgotten in the world to come. Beyond the peace that comes through gospel living and fellowship with the Saints, they will receive blessings unnumbered. The Lord knows his people and generously rewards—in this life and the next—those who give up something good for something essential. To receive such eternal rewards, we must maintain our hope in Christ: "Wherefore man must hope, or he cannot receive an inheritance in the place which thou hast prepared" (Ether 12:32). With regard to everlasting things, the faithful will lack for nothing.

And when they came that were hired about the eleventh hour,
they received every man a penny. But when they first came,
they supposed that they should have received more;
and they likewise received every man a penny.
—MATTHEW 20:9–10

 We do not obtain our heavenly reward by punch-
ing a time clock," Elder Dallin H. Oaks taught. "What
is essential is that our labors in the workplace of the
Lord have caused us to *become* something. For some of
us, this requires a longer time than for others. What
is important in the end is what we have become by our
labors. Many who come in the eleventh hour have
been refined and prepared by the Lord in ways other
than formal employment in the vineyard. These workers are like the prepared dry mix to which it is only
necessary to 'add water'—the perfecting ordinance of
baptism and the gift of the Holy Ghost. With that
addition—even in the eleventh hour—these workers
are . . . qualified to receive the same reward as those
who have labored long in the vineyard" (*Ensign*,
November 2000, 34). The gospel of Jesus Christ
is indeed a message of mercy and grace. We are
redeemed through the righteousness of our Savior.

And when Jesus came to the place, he looked up, and said unto him, Zacchaeus, make haste, and come down; for to day I must abide at thy house. And he made haste, and came down, and received him joyfully.

—LUKE 19:5–6

Jesus seeks and saves repentant souls. He came to find the lost and wandering, to bring the sanctifying power of his gospel to those bound by the chains of sin, to pour his love and light upon all who embrace the great plan of happiness. Jesus knows the desires of our hearts. His summons to repent and his offer of salvation is extended to all: "Behold, I stand at the door, and knock: if any man hear my voice, and open the door, I will come in to him, and will sup with him, and he with me" (Revelation 3:20). If, like Zacchaeus, we do not procrastinate but quickly respond to the Master's call (Alma 13:27; 34:35; Helaman 13:38), we can receive him joyfully, filling our souls with faith and our life with service in his kingdom. With love unbounded, we will welcome the Savior into our hearts and homes.

*And when [Jesus] saw a fig tree in the way, he came to it,
and found nothing thereon, but leaves only, and said unto it,
Let no fruit grow on thee henceforward for ever.
And presently the fig tree withered away.*
—MATTHEW 21:19

Those acquainted with fig trees know that leaves on the tree signal to the hungry that fruit is ready for picking. Despite its leaves, the tree spoken of in Matthew 21 was barren of fruit. Jesus' curse on the fig tree represents a curse upon those who exercised authority over the temple and the people of Israel, who professed to glory in the prophets of the past but rejected current revelation and the living word of God. "And all they who receive the oracles of God, let them beware how they hold them lest they are accounted as a light thing, and are brought under condemnation thereby, and stumble and fall when the storms descend, and the winds blow, and the rains descend, and beat upon their house" (D&C 90:5).

JULY

Her sins, which are many, are
forgiven; for she loved much:
but to whom little is forgiven,
the same loveth little.

—LUKE 7:47

And Jesus went into the temple of God, and cast out all them that
sold and bought in the temple, and overthrew the tables of the
moneychangers, and the seats of them that sold doves.
—MATTHEW 21:12

At the beginning of the Savior's public ministry
(John 2:13–17) and then in the final week of his mortal life, Jesus cleansed the temple by driving thieves,
merchants, and moneychangers from its walls. With
righteous indignation he exercised divine right to
sanctify his Father's house. He who was perfect in
every way, he who was gentle and kind, had his wrath
kindled by the misuse of the temple, and he even used
physical force to cleanse it. Such intensity points to the
sanctity of that holy house. The temple is a special
place of learning, prayer, and worship, separate from
the world. Though we would never set up shop in the
temple today, we may unwittingly bring the world into
the temple with us. We too must rid ourselves of
worldly preoccupation and cleanse our souls to perform with singleness of heart the ordinances of the
house of the Lord.

A certain man had two sons; and he came to the first, and said, Son, go work to day in my vineyard. He answered and said, I will not: but afterward he repented, and went. And he came to the second, and said likewise. And he answered and said, I go, sir: and went not. Whether of them twain did the will of his father?

—MATTHEW 21:28–31

We might wonder why Jesus' story of the man and his two sons "does not include a third son who said, 'I will,' and kept his word. Perhaps it is because this story characterizes humanity, and we all fall short (Romans 3:23). Thus Jesus could describe only two kinds of religious people: those who pretend to be obedient but are actually rebels, and those who begin as rebels but repent" (MacArthur, *Gospel According to Jesus,* 183–84). In fact, one of the signs of spiritual maturity is an earnest expression of weakness, an acknowledgment of the sins which so easily beset us, as well as a confession of him in whom we must trust (2 Nephi 4:18–19).

*What thinkest thou? Is it lawful to give tribute unto Caesar,
or not? . . . Then saith he unto them, Render therefore
unto Caesar the things which are Caesar's;
and unto God the things that are God's.*

—MATTHEW 22:17–21

We are subject to two powers—one the empire of earth and the other the kingdom of heaven. We are taught to obey, honor, and sustain the law (Articles of Faith 1:12), yet when he was asked, "Which is the great commandment in the law? Jesus said . . . Thou shalt love the Lord thy God with all thy heart, and with all thy soul" (Matthew 22:36–37). Elder Howard W. Hunter explained: "The image of monarchs stamped on coins denotes that temporal things belong to the temporal sovereign. The image of God stamped on the heart and soul of a man denotes that all its facilities and powers belong to God and should be employed in his service" (Conference Report, April 1968, 65). As children of God, we are each stamped with his image. We are to render unto him our will, our lives, even our hearts and souls.

Jesus answered and said unto them, Ye do err, not knowing the
scriptures, nor the power of God. For in the resurrection
they neither marry, nor are given in marriage,
but are as the angels of God in heaven.
—MATTHEW 22:29–30

Matthew 22 records Jesus teaching the Sadducees, a Jewish sect whose adherents denied life after death and the resurrection of the body. They obviously also rejected the Messiah and his gospel. But the Savior's teaching here also applies in a broader sense to all who reject the gospel and the power and authority to act in the name of God. None such can claim a bond between marriage partners that lasts beyond the grave. For example, if a woman who does not accept the restored gospel were to ask the president of the Church which of the men to whom she had been married would be her husband after death, his answer, of course, would be none of them. But just because one unbeliever has been told that none of her civil marriages is binding in eternity does not mean that the same is true for believers whose marriages are sealed in a holy temple by proper authority (D&C 132:15–20).

Master, which is the great commandment in the law? Jesus said
unto him, Thou shalt love the Lord thy God with all thy heart,
and with all thy soul, and with all thy mind. . . . And the
second is like unto it, Thou shalt love thy neighbour as thyself.
—MATTHEW 22:36–39

The Savior summarizes all of the Ten Commandments in the first and second great commandments. Simply put, the requirements for salvation can be traced to our responsibility to love God and our fellowmen. These loves cannot be separated. "If a man say, I love God, and hateth his brother, he is a liar: for he that loveth not his brother whom he hath seen, how can he love God whom he hath not seen?" (1 John 4:20). Love is measured daily in acts of service, sensitivity, and devotion. We are to love with all our hearts and souls (sincerity), our might (fervor), our mind (intelligent devotion), and our strength (energy and power). Jesus himself is an embodiment of the law of love, and upon him "hang all the law and the prophets" (Matthew 22:40).

And Jesus answered and said, while he taught in the temple,
How say the scribes that Christ is the Son of David?
For David himself . . . calleth him Lord;
and whence is he then his son?
—MARK 12:35–37

Isaiah and Abinadi taught that the Messiah was to be both Son and Father—the One who would condescend and leave his throne to dwell in the flesh among mortals and also the One who would possess the powers of glory and immortality. That is, the suffering Servant would eventually become King of kings and Lord of lords (Isaiah 53; Mosiah 14–15). The Jews in the meridian of time could not comprehend that the Messiah was to be both a literal descendant of King David and also the One who would reign triumphantly as Lord and King, the millennial David. Jesus taught John the Revelator, "I am the root and the offspring of David, and the bright and morning star" (Revelation 22:16). Because Jesus was a man, he knows of our challenges and struggles. Because he is God, he has the power to save us.

Woe unto you, scribes and Pharisees, hypocrites! for ye pay tithe
of mint and anise and cummin, and have omitted the weightier
matters of the law, judgment, mercy, and faith. . . . Ye blind
guides, which strain at a gnat, and swallow a camel.
—MATTHEW 23:23–24

Jesus reminds us that it is possible to live according to the outward mandates of a spiritual checklist and yet neglect the things that *really* matter, those which require changed and softened hearts. President James E. Faust has said: "Faithful members of the Church who are true to their covenants with the Master do not need every jot and tittle spelled out for them. Christlike conduct flows from the deepest well-springs of the human heart and soul. It is guided by the Holy Spirit of the Lord, which is promised in gospel ordinances. Our greatest hope should be to enjoy the sanctification which comes from this divine guidance; our greatest fear should be to forfeit these blessings. May we so live that we may be able to say, as did the Psalmist: 'Search me, O God, and know my heart'" (Conference Report, April 1998, 23).

Woe unto you, scribes and Pharisees, hypocrites! for ye
are like unto whited sepulchres, which indeed appear
beautiful outward, but are within full of dead
men's bones, and of all uncleannness.
—MATTHEW 23:27

President Joseph F. Smith is a good example of living without hypocrisy. Nine days before he died, he gathered his family together and said, "If there is anything on earth I have tried to do as much as anything else, it is to keep my word, my promises, my integrity, to do what it was my duty to do." Known for his integrity of heart, President Smith earlier had said, "The religion which we have espoused is not a Sunday religion; it is not a mere profession. . . . It is the most important thing in the world to us, and the results to us in this world and in the world to come will depend upon our integrity to the truth" (*Joseph F. Smith,* 416–17). How wonderful to have no façade of piety to hide inward wickedness—how wonderful to be able to meet one's Maker completely true to the truth.

*O Jerusalem, . . . how often would I have gathered thy
children together, even as a hen gathereth her
chickens under her wings, and ye would not!
Behold, your house is left unto you desolate.*
—MATTHEW 23:37–38

God seeks earnestly to gather his children to his gospel. They are gathered spiritually as they come unto Christ, accept his doctrine, and join his Church. Then they are gathered temporally as they meet in congregations of the faithful. They continue to grow spiritually from grace to grace until they are prepared to be endowed from on high in the house of the Lord. "What was the object of gathering the Jews, or the people of God in any age of the world?" asked the Prophet. "To build unto the Lord a house whereby He could reveal unto His people the ordinances of His house and the glories of His kingdom" (*Teachings of the Prophet Joseph Smith,* 307–8). The final phase of gathering thus entails receiving and observing the covenants and ordinances of the house of the Lord. Thereby we place ourselves in a position to have Christ "seal you his, that you may be brought to heaven, that ye may have everlasting salvation and eternal life" (Mosiah 5:15).

There came a certain poor widow, and she threw in two mites. . . .
And [Jesus] saith unto them, Verily I say unto you,
That this poor widow hath cast more in,
than all they which have cast into the treasury.
—MARK 12:42–43

In Jesus' day, a mite was a copper coin worth approximately one-eighth of a cent. Two mites were the equivalent of one-sixty-fourth of a day's wage. Rabbinic law specified that the smallest amount a person could deposit in the treasury was two mites. This poor widow gave the least that was permitted, but it was probably the most she could afford. From an eternal perspective, her paltry offering was worth more than the surplus of those who give in order to be seen of men. When it costs us but little to give, our eternal reward is a small one. Too often we judge a person's success by his or her income and possessions. Likewise, too often we judge a person's contribution by its monetary value. But the Omniscient One sees things differently: he looks upon the heart (1 Samuel 16:7). When we give with a pure and honest heart, that is all that is expected.

Verily, verily, I say unto you, Except a [grain] of wheat
fall into the ground and die, it abideth alone:
but if it die, it bringeth forth much fruit.
—JOHN 12:24

Jesus knew that his death was a vital part of his atoning sacrifice, that only as he submitted to torture and the cross would he be in a position to consummate his condescension. Pondering his approaching ordeal, he said, "Now is my soul troubled; and what shall I say? Father, save me from this hour: but for this cause came I unto this hour" (John 12:27). Centuries earlier, the Lord Jehovah spoke to Abraham of His messianic suffering: "The day cometh, that the Son of Man shall live; but how can he live if he be not dead? he must first be quickened" (JST Genesis 15:11). Jesus' rise to triumphant glory in the resurrection was preceded of necessity by his descent into unspeakable suffering and death. Only by descending below all things could he ascend above all things.

Now is the judgment of this world: now shall the prince of this world be cast out. And I, if I be lifted up from the earth, will draw all men unto me.

—JOHN 12:31–32

The mission of Jesus Christ signals the beginning of the end for Lucifer, the son of the morning, the "prince of this world." Through the Atonement, men and women are reconciled to the Father, renewed in spirit, and redeemed from endless torment. The One unto whom all judgment has been committed (John 5:22), the Holy One of Israel and Keeper of the gate (2 Nephi 9:41), came into the world that we estranged mortals might be reinstated into the royal family. As the risen Lord taught, "My Father sent me that I might be lifted up on the cross; and after that I had been lifted up upon the cross, that I might draw all men unto me, that as I have been lifted up by men even so should men be lifted up by the Father, to stand before me, to be judged of their works" (3 Nephi 27:14).

Jesus cried and said, He that believeth on me,
believeth not on me, but on him that sent me.
—JOHN 12:44

Jesus leads us to the Father—his Father and ours. When we believe and follow Jesus, we believe and follow God the Father. They are one. As the Prophet Joseph Smith taught, "The Father and Son [possess] the same mind, the same wisdom, glory, power, and fullness—filling all in all; the Son being filled with the fullness of the mind, glory, and power; or, in other words, the spirit, glory and power, of the Father, possessing all knowledge and glory, and the same kingdom, sitting at the right hand of power, in the express image and likeness of the Father, mediator for man, being filled with the fullness of the mind of the Father; or, in other words, the Spirit of the Father, which Spirit is shed forth upon all who believe on his name and keep his commandments" (*Lectures on Faith* 5:2). In short, to have faith in the Son is to have faith in the Father. Theirs is an everlasting oneness.

Nevertheless among the chief rulers also many believed on him;
but because of the Pharisees they did not confess him, lest
they should be put out of the synagogue: For they loved
the praise of men more than the praise of God.
—JOHN 12:42–43

Loving the praise of God more than the praise of men is central to our happiness and even to our salvation. President Gordon B. Hinckley warned that the twin traps of praise and prominence have ambushed countless men and women. "'Few people can bear the burden of notoriety,'" he has said. To a group of young adults he pleaded: "'Be humble. Don't be arrogant. . . . The world is full of arrogant people. How obnoxious is an arrogant man!'" (Dew, *Go Forward with Faith,* 512). The most meaningful praise we can receive is the peaceful assurance we get through the Spirit from doing what is right.

*Take heed that no man deceive you. For many shall come in my
name, saying, I am Christ; and shall deceive many.*
—MATTHEW 24:4–5

Not many people claim to be the returning King of
kings, and it is easy to discern that those few who do
are not who they claim to be. When the Lord speaks
of false Christs, therefore, he refers to false systems of
salvation, philosophical or religious methods that
promise association with God or life in the highest
heaven but are based on error and deceit. The wisdom
that flows from searching "diligently in the light of
Christ" (Moroni 7:19) enables us tell the difference.
"Wherefore, be not deceived," the Master said in a
modern revelation, "but continue in steadfastness,
looking forth for the heavens to be shaken, and the
earth to tremble and to reel to and fro as a drunken
man, and for the valleys to be exalted, and for the
mountains to be made low, and for the rough places to
become smooth" (D&C 49:23).

And because iniquity shall abound,
the love of many shall wax cold.
—MATTHEW 24:12

Love is a priceless virtue, but it can survive only in the heart of one who attempts to be true to what he or she knows is right. Alma counseled: "See that ye bridle all your passions, that ye may be filled with love" (Alma 38:12). Lust leads to loneliness. Unbridled passions are followed by fear. "He that looketh on a woman to lust after her . . . shall not have the Spirit, but shall deny the faith and shall fear" (D&C 63:16). Fear. Fear of being found out, fear of rejection, fear of facing the vainness of one's own life. But if we are filled with the love of Christ we do not waste our life in worry or ache with anxiety about the future. The love of Christ brings peace and contentment. As John taught, "There is no fear in love; but perfect love casteth out fear" (1 John 4:18).

But he that shall endure unto the end, the same shall be saved.
—MATTHEW 24:13

Enduring to the end" has been called the fifth principle of the gospel. We enter into covenant with Christ through baptism, but it is not enough to be born again in a single instance, changed in a moment. Real gospel living requires daily commitment thereafter. We continue on the gospel path, day by day doing our best to overcome, grow, learn, obey, and serve. We engage in a lifelong process of spiritual rebirth by persevering with immovable faith in the Savior. If we remain faithful, we will be saved from the destruction of the wicked and will enter into the kingdom of heaven.

And this gospel of the kingdom shall be preached in all the world
for a witness unto all nations; and then shall the end come.
—MATTHEW 24:14

Prophets have testified that the gospel is to be preached to every nation, kindred, tongue, and people before the Lord returns in glory. This marvelous work began in the spring of 1820 when young Joseph Smith entered a grove of trees and humbly sought an answer to a prayer. The Father and the Son appeared, new scripture came forth, divine authority was conferred, the Church was organized, and God distilled doctrine and truth upon the earth. The knowledge of a restored Church of Jesus Christ with all the keys, saving ordinances, and transcendent truths necessary for the salvation of man is the most vital message we can share. As we witness to the world that Jesus Christ is our Savior and will again rule and reign on the earth, we also bear witness to the restoration of his Church.

For wheresoever the carcase is,
there will the eagles be gathered together.
—MATTHEW 24:28

Vultures circling overhead are a pretty good sign that something has died or is about to die. Similarly, when we notice that the gathering of Israel has intensified—when people begin to receive the message of the Restoration and come into the Church by baptism in greater and greater numbers—we may be assured that we are being shown another of the Master's signs incident to his second coming. Speaking of the manner in which his second advent will cause "an entire separation of the righteous and the wicked" (D&C 63:54; 2 Nephi 30:10) and thus the ultimate death of wickedness, Jesus said, "Wheresoever the body is gathered; or, in other words, whithersoever the saints are gathered; thither will the eagles be gathered together; or, thither will the remainder be gathered together" (JST Luke 17:37).

But of that day and hour knoweth no man, no,
not the angels of heaven, but my Father only.
—MATTHEW 24:36

President Joseph Fielding Smith taught regarding the Savior's second coming: "The signs that have been pointed out are here. . . . We see the signs as we see the fig tree putting forth her leaves; and knowing this time is near, it behooves me and it behooves you, and all men upon the face of the earth, to pay heed to the words of Christ, to his apostles and watch, for we know not the day nor the hour. But I tell you this, it shall come as a thief in the night, when many of us will not be ready for it" (*Doctrines of Salvation*, 3:52–53). Though the Saints know not the day or the hour, those who are in tune with the Spirit and give heed to the living oracles will be aware of the season. We are to treasure up the Lord's word so we will not be deceived, and so we can spiritually prepare for the return of Jesus.

They were eating and drinking, marrying and giving in marriage,
until the day that Noe entered into the ark,
and knew not until the flood came, and took them all away;
so shall also the coming of the Son of man be.
—MATTHEW 24:38–39

As the gathering is accelerated, the honest in heart will come into the true Church in ever-increasing numbers. The Church of the Lamb of God will spread its influence far and wide, and the Saints will be "armed with righteousness and with the power of God in great glory" (1 Nephi 14:14). At the same time, the forces of evil will be marshaled as the enemy combines and concentrates his nefarious purposes. While the worldly continue to go about their business—"eating and drinking, marrying and giving in marriage"— oblivious to the fulfillment of prophecy and insensitive to the warnings of the Lord's covenant spokesmen, those within the household of faith who cultivate the gift of the Holy Ghost will be blessed to recognize the signs of the times and will thus be able to prepare for the coming of the Son of Man.

*If the goodman of the house had known in what watch the
thief would come, he would have watched. . . . Therefore
be ye also ready: for in such an hour as ye think
not the Son of man cometh.*

—MATTHEW 24:43–44

To faithful members of the Church, the apostle Paul
wrote: "The day of the Lord so cometh as a thief in the
night. For when they shall say, Peace and safety; then
sudden destruction cometh upon them, as travail upon
a woman with child; and they shall not escape. But ye,
brethren, are not in darkness, that that day should
overtake you as a thief" (1 Thessalonians 5:2–4).
When a woman is nine months pregnant, she does not
know the exact moment when labor will begin, but she
does know one thing—the baby will be born soon!
The signs within her own body so attest. So it will be
with the members of the body of Christ. Those who
are in tune with the Spirit of God and listen to the
words of living prophets will read the signs of
the times and thereby know the season in which the
Master will return.

Then shall the kingdom of heaven be likened unto ten virgins,
which took their lamps, and went forth to meet the bridegroom.
And five of them were wise, and five were foolish.
—MATTHEW 25:1–2

In the timeless parable of the ten virgins, five of them were found without the fuel necessary to keep their lamps burning. They had not exercised enough foresight to prepare for what lay ahead, and when the crucial moment arrived, it was too late to prepare. Some things one simply cannot borrow at the last minute. Just as the virgins' small lamps required a careful and methodical effort to be filled, so our reservoirs of faith and spiritual depth need to be built gradually, drop by tiny drop. Every noble deed, every prayer, every period of sincere fasting, every testimony borne, every moment of reflection adds to the reservoir. Too many seek desperately, at a time of crisis, to compensate for long-term neglect through sudden bursts of effort. Jesus taught that the way to peace and preparation is not through spiritual marathons at the last hour but through consistent, lifelong personal progress.

His lord said unto him, Well done, thou good and faithful servant:
thou hast been faithful over a few things, I will make thee ruler
over many things: enter thou into the joy of thy lord.
—MATTHEW 25:21

We reap what we sow, both temporally and spiritually. No reward or growth comes from cramming or shortcuts. The law of the harvest teaches that when we do our part "and serve him with all [our] heart, might, mind and strength" (D&C 4:2), we will reap the glories promised faithful Saints (D&C 132:19). Our loving God wants for us all that he has if we will but do our part with full purpose of heart (Luke 15:31). What greater promise, what more magnificent gift could be extended to us by the Lord than to have our good works honored, mercy extended, and our reward enlarged. We all labor in limited spheres here in mortality, but how comforting it is to know that when we are faithful, our "few things" will be added upon.

Then he which had received the one talent came and said, Lord,
I knew thee that thou art an hard man, . . . and I was afraid,
and went and hid thy talent in the earth.
—MATTHEW 25:24–25

In the parable of the talents, Jesus admonishes us to enlarge upon our abilities and use our every talent in the Lord's service. Although perfection is pending, this life is the time to strive to become all that God wants us to be. Either we progress with faith and courage or wither and die from fear and laziness. Elder James E. Talmage wrote: "The honest, diligent, faithful servants saw and reverenced in their Lord the perfection of the good qualities which they possessed in measured degree; the lazy and unprofitable serf, afflicted by distorted vision, professed to see in the Master his own base defects. . . . In a peculiar sense men are prone to conceive of the attributes of God as comprising in augmented degree the dominant traits of their own nature" (*Jesus the Christ*, 582). While we are called to fear God, in the sense of demonstrating reverence and respect toward the Almighty, a morbid and unhealthy fear of God's wrath stifles growth and frustrates our spiritual development.

Verily I say unto you, Inasmuch as ye have done it unto one of the least of these my brethren, ye have done it unto me.
—MATTHEW 25:40

As we serve our fellow beings with love, we are truly loving and serving our God. In a world that is increasingly more complex and technological, it's easy to lose the warmth of the human touch. The only way to counteract the dehumanizing aspects of our world is to make conscious efforts to build bonds of love. Our time and concern are among the most precious gifts we can offer. In these lines from *The Vision of Sir Launfal,* James Russell Lowell describes, from the Lord's perspective, the vital power of reaching out in love and service:

> Not what we give, but what we share—
> For the gift without the giver is bare.
> Who gives himself with his alms serves three—
> Himself, his hungering neighbor, and me.

*He took bread, and gave thanks, and brake it, and gave unto them,
saying, This is my body which is given for you: this do in
remembrance of me. Likewise also the cup . . . saying,
This cup is the new testament in my blood, which is shed for you.*
—LUKE 22:19–20

While teaching his apostles in their last formal gathering before his ordeal, the Savior instituted the sacrament of the Lord's supper. The sacrament is an ordinance of salvation, a means by which a gracious God can cleanse and endow and empower his covenant people. It provides for us a moment of introspection, a time for renewal, a period of recommitment to him whose body was broken and whose blood was spilt for us in the greatest act of mercy and love ever manifest. The sacrament enables us to become one with Christ. As the resurrected Lord said to his Nephite followers, "He that eateth this bread eateth of my body to his soul; and he that drinketh of this wine drinketh of my blood to his soul; and his soul shall never hunger nor thirst, but shall be filled" (3 Nephi 20:8).

He riseth from supper, and laid aside his garments; and took a towel, and girded himself. After that he poureth water into a bason, and began to wash the disciples' feet, and to wipe them with the towel wherewith he was girded.

—JOHN 13:4–5

Never did the Savior give in expectation," President Spencer W. Kimball declared. "I know of no case in his life in which there was an exchange. He was always the giver, seldom the recipient. . . . His gifts were of such a nature that the recipient could hardly exchange or return the value. His gifts were rare ones: eyes to the blind, ears to the deaf, and legs to the lame; cleanliness to the unclean, wholeness to the infirm, and breath to the lifeless. His gifts were opportunity to the downtrodden, freedom to the oppressed, light in the darkness, forgiveness to the repentant, hope to the despairing. His friends gave him shelter, food, and love. He gave them of himself, his love, his service, his life" (*Teachings of Spencer W. Kimball,* 246–47). We are called to give as he gave—to give of ourselves to others.

As they did eat [at the Last Supper], he said,
Verily I say unto you, that one of you shall betray me.
And they were exceeding sorrowful,
and began every one of them to say unto him, Lord, is it I?
—MATTHEW 26:21–22

It is a tribute to the nobility of the men chosen by the Lord as apostles that they did not sound off in accusatory fashion to confess another man's sins. The temptation was surely great to whisper: "I know who it is; it's Judas Iscariot. He's been acting strange lately." Or, "You know, Simon Peter has seemed a bit squeamish during the past few days. I wonder if he's the one." Instead, the word of the Master sobered them, leading each of the eleven apostles to engage in serious introspection. "Search your hearts," the Prophet Joseph Smith implored us, "and see if you are like God. I have searched mine, and feel to repent of all my sins" (*Teachings of the Prophet Joseph Smith,* 216).

A new commandment I give unto you, That ye love one another;
as I have loved you, that ye also love one another.
By this shall all men know that ye are my disciples,
if ye have love one to another.

—JOHN 13:34–35

There is much misunderstanding in the world today regarding the God of the Bible. Some believe that the God of the Old Testament is a vengeful being who seems to delight in punishing the frailties of humankind, while Jesus of the New Testament is the compassionate Savior of the world. In fact, the God of the Old Testament is the very same being as the God of the New Testament: Jehovah is Christ, and his divine attributes, including his infinite capacity to love, are forever the same. It was the God of the Old Testament who said: "Thou shalt love thy neighbour as thyself: I am the Lord" (Leviticus 19:18). Jesus' "new commandment" was new only in the sense that it was now being given an emphasis that it had never received before. It is the synthesis of all the commandments, truly the "royal law" (James 2:8).

*And the Lord said, Simon, Simon, behold, Satan hath desired to
have you, that he may sift you as wheat: But I have prayed
for thee, that thy faith fail not: and when thou art
converted, strengthen thy brethren.*

—LUKE 22:31–32

Satan knew that if Peter fell and was not there to guide the meridian Saints, there would be a better chance of disrupting the spread of the Church. In consequence, Jesus prayed that Peter's faith would not fail. Today, we have the privilege of praying for the apostles and prophets that they will be strengthened and protected. One of the ways we demonstrate our conversion is to follow their counsel. As we do so, we will be changed from carnal, worldly individuals to beings of saintliness and righteousness. We will proceed along the path of true conversion. True converts change their whole way of life and are transformed by the power of the Holy Ghost (Mosiah 5:2). If we are to strengthen ourselves and others against the cunning plan of the evil one, we must truly be converted.

AUGUST

Whosoever drinketh of the
water that I shall give him shall
never thirst; but the water that I
shall give him shall be in him a
well of water springing up
into everlasting life.

—JOHN 4:14

*In my Father's house are many mansions: if it were not so,
I would have told you. I go to prepare a place for you.*
—JOHN 14:2

Joseph Smith explained: "It appeared self-evident from what truths were left [in the Bible], that if God rewarded every one according to the deeds done in the body, the term 'Heaven,' as intended for the Saints' eternal home, must include more kingdoms than one" (D&C 76, headnote). The Prophet and Sidney Rigdon then received the vision of the glories, a magnificent revelation that serves as a kind of doctrinal commentary upon the Savior's words recorded in John 14:2. It is as though Jesus had said to his apostles, "The idea that God will reward every person according to his or her own faith and righteousness is so obvious that if it were not so, I would have told you!" In other words, God's great plan of happiness is a personal system of salvation.

Jesus saith unto him, I am the way, the truth, and the life: no man cometh unto the Father, but by me.
—JOHN 14:6

Christ is *the* way. To come unto the Father we must follow Christ and walk in his paths. "Follow thou me," he commands (2 Nephi 31:10). He is *the* truth. His word is truth, he knows all truth, has all truth, and is all truth; his truth sets us free (John 8:32). "I am the Spirit of truth," he instructs (D&C 93:26; John 17:17). He is *the* life. He is our Redeemer who saves us from spiritual and temporal death. "In him was life; and the life was the light of men" (John 1:4). "We can find a perfect example in the life of Jesus," said President David O. McKay. "Whatsoever our noble desires, our lofty aspirations, our ideals in any phase of life, we can look to Christ and find perfection" (Conference Report, April 1968, 6–7).

*Philip saith unto him, Lord, shew us the Father,
and it sufficeth us. Jesus saith unto him, Have I been so long time
with you, and yet hast thou not known me, Philip?
he that hath seen me hath seen the Father.*
—JOHN 14:8–9

Among the central truths of the gospel is the knowledge that our Heavenly Father is an exalted man with a body of flesh and bones (D&C 130:22) and that we are created in his image. A parallel preeminent truth is that Jesus Christ is his Only Begotten Son in the flesh. He and the Father are separate personages, and yet they are one in purpose, glory, and attributes. After completing the infinite atoning sacrifice, Jesus received all power in heaven and in earth; he received the fulness of the glory of the Father (Matthew 28:18; D&C 93:16). The Father and Son thus possess "the same mind, the same wisdom, glory, power, and fullness" (Smith, *Lectures on Faith* 5:2). To obey the Son is to obey the Father. To honor the Son is to honor the Father. And, in a very real sense, to see the Son is to see the Father.

Believest thou not that I am in the Father, and the Father
in me? the words that I speak unto you I speak not
of myself: but the Father that dwelleth in me,
he doeth the works.
—JOHN 14:10

Jesus lived and moved and had his being in the Spirit of God, "for God giveth him not the Spirit by measure, for he dwelleth in him, even the fulness" (JST John 3:34). While the New Testament affirms that the Son was subordinate to his Father in mortality (John 4:34; 5:19, 30; 6:38–40; 14:28), the Father and the Son enjoyed much more than closeness; theirs was a divine, indwelling relationship. Because he kept the law of God, Jesus was in the Father, and the Father was in him (John 14:10, 20; 17:21; 1 John 3:24). In like manner, we are under commission to strive to be one with God, to have, as Paul wrote, "the mind of Christ" (1 Corinthians 2:16). We gain the mind of Christ as Christ gained the mind of the Father—through the power of the Spirit.

Verily, verily, I say unto you, He that believeth on me,
the works that I do shall he do also;
and greater works than these shall he do.
—JOHN 14:12

Jesus is not the kind of leader who essentially says to his disciples, "Catch me if you can," but rather one who invites us to "Come, follow me." Nor is the Master possessive about his powers or unwilling to share the benefits and blessings of the gospel with any who desire to partake. True servants of Christ do the works of Christ. He worshipped his Father; so do they. He taught the gospel; so do they. He went about doing good; so do they. He performed miracles; so do they. He served and ministered in mortality and then in the postmortal spirit world; so do they.

If ye love me, keep my commandments.
—JOHN 14:15

We manifest true love by our devotion to God. Love is the very essence of the gospel of Jesus Christ. It is the gospel's most vital verb; it implies action. Love is demonstrated through service (D&C 59:5–6) and manifest through obedience. Do we obey because of our deep love and devotion to God? Or do we obey for lesser, even selfish, reasons? Those who truly love God with heart, soul, and might humbly place their will upon the Lord's altar. Love of God is manifest among those who love God's children. We cannot say we love God and hate (or belittle, denigrate, or wish ill upon) others. If we love God, we sincerely strive to have love in our hearts for *all* of his children. "And this commandment have we from him, That he who loveth God love his brother also" (1 John 4:21).

*And I will pray the Father, and he shall give you another
Comforter, that he may abide with you for ever;
even the Spirit of truth; whom the world cannot receive,
because it seeth him not, neither knoweth him.*

—JOHN 14:16–17

For three years Jesus had been the Apostles' Comforter. He now tells the disciples that once he has left their midst he will send them "another Comforter." The word *another* means one of the same kind, someone like the Lord himself who will teach and empower them. The Greek word translated in the Bible as "Comforter" means literally "one called to stand along side of." Other meanings include a friend, a counselor, a defender, a helper, and even an advocate. While ultimately Christ is our Advocate with the Father (D&C 45:3–5), the Savior has sent his Spirit to convict us of sin, convince us of the truth, and direct us toward righteousness (John 16:8–11). By means of the powers of the Spirit, men and women gain the witness of the divinity of Jesus Christ and come to know the things of eternity (1 Corinthians 12:3; 14:25–26).

But the Comforter, which is the Holy Ghost, whom the
Father will send in my name, he shall teach you all
things, and bring all things to your remembrance,
whatsoever I have said unto you.

—JOHN 14:26

Jesus promised to send his disciples the Holy Ghost to teach and help them after he left. It is by the Holy Ghost that we "know the truth of all things" (Moroni 10:5); it is by this Comforter that he whispers peace to our souls (D&C 6:23; 1 Kings 19:12). President Gordon B. Hinckley has stated: "There is no greater blessing that can come into our lives than the gift of the Holy Ghost—the companionship of the Holy Spirit to guide us, protect us, and bless us, to go, as it were, as a pillar before us and a flame to lead us in paths of righteousness and truth. That guiding power of the third member of the Godhead can be ours if we live worthy of it" (*Teachings of Gordon B. Hinckley,* 259).

Peace I leave with you, my peace I give unto you:
not as the world giveth, give I unto you.
Let not your heart be troubled, neither let it be afraid.
—JOHN 14:27

Peace comes when our actions reflect our deepest values. Lasting peace, the peace "which passeth all understanding" (Philippians 4:7), comes from turning our hearts to God. This peace helps us not only through the dark valleys of worry and pain but also through dimly lit passages of our daily lives. This peace, most treasured, is God's promise to each of us. President Brigham Young stated: "There is no real peace, there is no real happiness in anything in heaven or on the earth, except to those who serve the Lord. In his service there is joy, there is happiness; but they are not to be found anywhere else. In it there are peace and comfort. . . . But when a person is filled with the peace and power of God, all is right with him" (*Journal of Discourses* 5:1–2).

*I am the vine, ye are the branches: He that abideth in me,
and I in him, the same bringeth forth much fruit:
for without me ye can do nothing.*
—JOHN 15:5

Only as the Lord assists us are we able to bring to pass great things. One writer noted, "If you do not learn to abide in Christ, you will never have a marriage characterized by love, joy, and peace. You will never have the self-control necessary to consistently overcome temptation. And you will always be an emotional hostage of your circumstances. Why? Because apart from abiding in Christ, you can do nothing. . . . He is the vine; we are the branches. The two are joined, but not one. The common denominator in nature is the sap. The sap is the life of the vine and its branches. Cut off the flow of the sap to the branch, and it slowly withers and dies. As the branch draws its life from the vine, so we draw life from Christ. To abide in Christ is to draw upon His life" (Stanley, *Wonderful, Spirit-Filled Life,* 64).

*This is my commandment, That ye love one another,
as I have loved you. Greater love hath no man than this,
that a man lay down his life for his friends. Ye are my friends, if
ye do whatsoever I command you.*
—JOHN 15:12–14

Bruce and Marie Hafen have written that the Savior's "friends are those for whom he made the atoning sacrifice, not only by laying down his life but also by paying for their sins and bearing the burden of their infirmities: 'Ye are they whom my Father hath given me; ye are my friends.' (D&C 84:63.) Part of Christ's sacrifice benefits his enemies as well as his friends; but only his friends obey him enough to receive the fulness of his blessings. His friends are thus those who keep the covenants they made at baptism and then renew those covenants continually through the relationship of belonging to Christ. Moreover, they keep not only his general commandments but all of the covenants that arise from coming to Christ" (Hafen and Hafen, *Belonging Heart*, 155–56).

Ye have not chosen me, but I have chosen you,
and ordained you, that ye should go and bring forth fruit,
and that your fruit should remain.
—JOHN 15:16

Paul said, "No man taketh this honour unto himself, but he that is called of God, as was Aaron" (Hebrews 5:4). The Lord chooses his ministers, who then have the holy priesthood conferred upon them and are ordained by the laying on of hands (Articles of Faith 1:5). "Try to imagine if you can, being 'called' by the Master and 'ordained' under His hands," said Elder Harold B. Lee. "That these ordinations resulted in an endowment of power from on high as well as giving authority to act officially as the Lord's representatives, is well attested by the miraculous events that followed, which made of them, 'men different' because of that divine commission. Not alone were these special apostolic witnesses to receive and enjoy these heavenly gifts. They were commissioned to transmit them by ordinations to others who had received the witness of the divine mission of the risen Lord" (Conference Report, April 1955, 18–19).

It is expedient for you that I go away:
for if I go not away,
the Comforter will not come unto you.
—JOHN 16:7

The full gifts of the Holy Ghost were not given in the meridian Church until the day of Pentecost. While the Bridegroom was present with his disciples in the flesh, he was their Comforter and Revelator. But the Holy Spirit would play a vital role thereafter in the expansion of the early Christian Church. Christ "declared that the manifestations we might have of . . . an angel, a tangible resurrected being, would not leave the impression and would not convince us and place within us that something which we cannot get away from which we receive through a manifestation of the Holy Ghost. Personal visitations might become dim as time goes on, but this guidance of the Holy Ghost is renewed and continued, day after day, year after year, if we live to be worthy of it" (Smith, *Doctrines of Salvation,* 1:44).

*These things I have spoken unto you, that in me ye might have
peace. In the world ye shall have tribulation:
but be of good cheer; I have overcome the world.*
—JOHN 16:33

So much of life is troublesome. At times we feel
overwhelmed with worry; we wonder about the present or are fearful about the future. We may feel that
peace eludes us. Some search for peace on the dead-
end streets of selfishness or take unsatisfying detours
through empty fields of pleasure. Usually, they return
to where they started and feel the same turmoil they
felt before their momentary reprieve. To feel real
peace, the kind that carries us through difficult times,
we must draw near to the Prince of Peace. Jesus'
promise is real. Those who obey his commandments
feel his comforting influence in their hearts, and they
are not afraid. In the face of every peril, they can pray
to God. He will answer by the still, small voice of
the Holy Spirit and speak peace to their souls. This
is the peace "which passeth all understanding"
(Philippians 4:7).

And this is life eternal, that they might know thee the only true God, and Jesus Christ, whom thou has sent.

—JOHN 17:3

Jesus explained that at the day of judgment many will "say unto me . . . Lord, Lord, have we not prophesied in thy name; and in thy name cast out devils; and in thy name done many wonderful works? And then will I say, Ye never knew me; depart from me ye that work iniquity" (JST Matthew 7:32–33). Those who will qualify for eternal life are those who know God. They will know him because they will have been redeemed from their sins (Mosiah 26:24–26). They will know him because they will have "the mind of Christ" (1 Corinthians 2:16), having cultivated the gift and gifts of the Holy Ghost. They will know him because they will have surrendered their hearts to him. They will know him because, having become like him, they see him as he is (1 John 3:2).

I have glorified thee on the earth:
I have finished the work which thou gavest me to do.
—JOHN 17:4

These words are part of the Master's intercessory prayer. The work of atonement was about to begin in the Garden of Gethsemane and would be consummated on the cross the next day. In a very real way, Jesus' life of service and sacrifice and healing and training was at a close. He had gone forth "amongst men, working mighty miracles, such as healing the sick, raising the dead, causing the lame to walk, the blind to receive their sight, and the deaf to hear." He had "cast out devils, or the evil spirits which dwell in the hearts of the children of men." He had suffered "temptation, and pain of body, hunger, thirst, and fatigue, even more than man can suffer, except it be unto death" (Mosiah 3:5–7). There but remained for him now to face the climax, the consummation of a matchless work, a perfect ministry.

I pray not that thou shouldest take them out of the world,
but that thou shouldest keep them from the evil.
—JOHN 17:15

In Jesus' magnificent intercessory prayer he pleads for our growth and protection. He who knows all things understands that we need both. We are here to gain experience, to be tested and tutored, and to prove ourselves worthy of a celestial inheritance. As we turn from evil and transform our hearts, we begin to transcend the world and fill the measure of our mortal creation. Safety comes from being clasped in the arms of Jesus (Mormon 5:11). It comes from seeking Jesus in humility and faith, in prayer and repentance (Matthew 7:7–8; 11:28–30). It comes from separating ourselves—our thoughts, hearts, and actions—from the world, and yet understanding that it is in the world that we learn and grow and develop the attributes of godliness. Even in the mires of mortality, our hearts can be elevated to the things of eternity as we turn to the Savior.

As thou hast sent me into the world, even so have I also sent them into the world. And for their sakes I sanctify myself, that they also might be sanctified through the truth.
—JOHN 17:18–19

Many a mother and father have been kept from sin by thinking of their beloved children. Into their minds comes the sobering thought: "My children look up to me. I cannot let them down." So often we choose the right because there are others who look to us as an example. That is, we do what is right and remain in the line of our duty because doing so proves a blessing to others. Leaders in the Church at every level know that their ability to direct and inspire those under their charge is inextricably tied to their own faithfulness and earnest efforts to remain aloof from the taints of this world. Like Jesus, we sanctify ourselves—meaning we yield our hearts to God and seek to have an eye single to his glory (Helaman 3:35; D&C 88:67–68)—so that the Lord can work his wonders through us.

Neither pray I for these alone, but for them also which shall
believe on me through their word; That they all may be one;
as thou, Father, art in me, and I in thee,
that they also may be one in us.
—JOHN 17:20–21

God's eternal command resounds in all dispensations: "Be one; and if ye are not one ye are not mine" (D&C 38:27). The perfect example of unity is the eternal Godhead. Though three separate, distinct Gods, they are one—one in characteristics, attributes, and purpose. We also are to be one—one in desire to build and uphold the kingdom of God on the earth; one in doctrinal truth and devotion to the gospel (3 Nephi 11:28); one in love and fellowship with the Saints where no division, envy, or malice is present (1 Corinthians 1:10). Sameness is not oneness. Uniformity is not unity. We are individual people with a range of interests, personalities, and foibles. But when it comes to the everlasting things of the kingdom, we are to become one with the Lord, one with his people—united in truth.

And when they had sung an hymn,
they went out into the mount of Olives.
—MARK 14:26

The singing of hymns is a wonderful way to soften our hearts and put us in tune with the Spirit of the Lord. The First Presidency has said: "The hymns . . . create a feeling of reverence, unify us as members, and provide a way for us to offer praises to the Lord. Some of the greatest sermons are preached by the singing of hymns" (*Hymns,* p. ix). In one of the earliest revelations given through the Prophet Joseph Smith, the Lord appointed Emma Smith "to make a selection of sacred hymns. . . . For my soul delighteth in the song of the heart; yea, the song of the righteous is a prayer unto me, and it shall be answered with a blessing upon their heads" (D&C 25:11–12).

*When Jesus had spoken these words, he went forth with his
disciples over the brook Cedron, where was a garden, into the
which he entered, and his disciples. And Judas also . . . knew the
place: for Jesus ofttimes resorted thither with his disciples.*
—JOHN 18:1–2

Elder Bruce R. McConkie spoke of Christ in Gethsemane: Two thousand years ago, outside Jerusalem's
walls, there was a pleasant garden spot, Gethsemane
by name, where Jesus and his intimate friends were
wont to retire for pondering and prayer. There Jesus
taught his disciples the doctrines of the kingdom, and
all of them communed with Him who is the Father of
us all, in whose ministry they were engaged, and on
whose errand they served. This sacred spot, like Eden
where Adam dwelt, like Sinai from whence Jehovah
gave his laws, like Calvary where the Son of God gave
his life a ransom for many, this holy ground is where
the Sinless Son of the Everlasting Father took upon
himself the sins of all men on condition of repentance" (Conference Report, April 1985, 9).

And he was withdrawn from them about a stone's cast,
and kneeled down, and prayed, saying, Father,
if thou be willing, remove this cup from me;
nevertheless, not my will, but thine, be done.
—LUKE 22:41–42

The words we sing at Christmastime seem even more appropriate for the night of atonement: "The hopes and fears of all the years are met in thee tonight" (*Hymns,* no. 208). Indeed, all of eternity hung in the balance as the Man of Nazareth began to take upon him the sins of all humankind. As the burden of sin began to weigh upon him, the Father withdrew his Spirit. That withdrawal, that alienation and agony, which Jesus had never known, caused him to sweat blood from every pore. The hours of Gethsemane were a period of bitter irony: he who had never taken a backward step or a moral detour now became "sin for us" (2 Corinthians 5:21; Hebrews 4:15). Having descended below all things, having "trodden the winepress alone" (D&C 76:107), Jesus won the victory.

Jesus said unto him, Judas,
betrayest thou the Son of man with a kiss?
—LUKE 22:48

A more traitorous token could not have been chosen," wrote Elder Bruce R. McConkie. "Among the prophets of old, among the saints of that day, and even among the Jews, a kiss was a symbol of that love and fellowship which existed where pure religion was or should have been found. . . . Judas, thus, could have chosen no baser means of identifying Jesus than to plant on his face a traitor's kiss" (*Doctrinal New Testament Commentary,* 1:781–82). Fueled by envy and ego, Judas traded his apostolic call for a few coins. "What shall a man give in exchange for his soul?" asked Jesus some six months before this egregious betrayal (Matthew 16:26). It is easy to point a finger at Judas, but perhaps we should examine our own hearts. Do we ever betray the Savior with a kiss of hollow intent? Do we serve him with all our hearts?

*One of them smote the servant of the high priest, and cut
off his right ear. And Jesus answered and said, Suffer ye
thus far. And he touched his ear, and healed him.*
—LUKE 22:50—51

Jesus had been betrayed, arrested, and bound as a
common criminal. He allowed himself to be taken so
as to fulfill the scriptures and drink the bitter cup the
Father had given him (Matthew 26:54; John 18:11). He
who could command twelve legions of angels—and
more—to rescue him (and to punish his persecutors)
would make no move to circumvent the course he
must follow. And now with encompassing love and
empathy he healed the high priest's servant, Malchus,
whose right ear was cut off by Peter. Jesus could have
let that act of vengeance pass, thinking it justified or
deserved. But he who was perfect at all times and in
all places was perfectly compassionate during these
culminating moments that led to the cruel cross.

The high priest asked him, . . . Art thou the Christ,
the Son of the Blessed? And Jesus said, I am:
and ye shall see the Son of man sitting on the right
hand of power, and coming in the clouds of heaven.
—MARK 14:61–62

For centuries men filled with doubt have suggested that Jesus never directly taught who he was—namely, the Son of God. To be sure, there were times when Jesus performed miracles and pleaded with the healed ones to keep the matter to themselves. There were also times when Jesus instructed his chosen disciples to "tell no man" that he was the Son of Man. Such an approach was a matter of timing; the Lord did not want to foster an outcry that would result in his arrest before his ministry had been accomplished. But there are too many testimonies in the four Gospels, too many "I Am" statements, too many allusions to his labors as fulfillment of prophecy for us to suppose some kind of messianic secret. Jesus knew who he was and told others. This was no secret then, and it is no secret today.

And some began to spit on him, and to cover his face, and to buffet
him, and to say unto him, Prophesy: and the servants
did strike him with the palms of their hands.
—MARK 14:65

Not only was Jesus falsely accused and lied about,
he was laughed at, scorned, slapped, and spit upon.
The cruel physical assaults accompanied by the mock-
ing sarcasm were but prelude to the horrors that lay
ahead. Jesus knew full well the ultimate conclusion.
He did all of this without ever looking back. What
courage, what love he manifested as he walked the
lonely road of atonement.

> *Sing praises to him who reigns above,*
> *The Lord of all creation,*
> *The source of pow'r, the fount of love,*
> *The rock of our salvation.*
> *With healing balm my soul he fills*
> *And ev'ry faithless murmur stills.*
> *To him all praise and glory!*
>
> (Hymns, no. 70)

And when she saw Peter warming himself, she looked upon him, and said, And thou also wast with Jesus of Nazareth. But he denied, saying, I know not, neither understand I what thou sayest. And he went out into the porch; and the cock crew.
—MARK 14:67–68

Elder Spencer W. Kimball suggested that we use caution before condemning Simon Peter for his denial of Jesus. For one thing, Peter did not really deny Christ; he denied knowing him. Secondly, fear of arrest or even of death seems inconsistent for Peter; only hours earlier he had cut off the ear of a servant in the Garden of Gethsemane in a brave effort to defend his Lord. Finally, there may be more to the story than our brief account provides. Was Peter's denial of his own volition, or had the Master instructed him to do it? What if Peter had fought back, lashed out against the leaders of the Jews? If Peter were arrested, who would have led the young church? (*Teachings of Spencer W. Kimball*, 470–72). In this, as in so many of life's circumstances, we would do well to follow the Savior's counsel that we "judge not, that ye be not judged" (Matthew 7:1).

Jesus answered, My kingdom is not of this world:
if my kingdom were of this world, then would my servants fight,
that I should not be delivered to the Jews:
but now is my kingdom not from hence.
—JOHN 18:36

For centuries the Jews had longed for the day when a powerful king would arise and deliver them from the oppression of their alien overlords. Jesus of Nazareth came into the world to deliver, not just the Jews, but all men and women. Jesus had the right, by foreordination and lineal Davidic descent, to rule and reign as the King of the Jews. But the people of his day were not, on the whole, prepared to receive him. Truly, he came unto his own, and his own received him not (John 1:11). Jesus spoke of repentance rather than revolution, of divine surrender rather than military victory. Indeed, the kingdom of Jesus Christ was not of this fallen world, and it would not be fully established until the great millennial day when "he reigns whose right it is to reign" (D&C 58:22).

*Jesus answered, Thou sayest that I am a king. To this end
was I born, and for this cause came I into the world,
that I should bear witness unto the truth.
Every one that is of the truth heareth my voice.*
—JOHN 18:37

Jesus reveals what we might call his mission statement: he is come into the world to bring truth. As the
embodiment of truth—as *the* Truth—he bears witness
that the honest in heart will know him as such (John
10:27). Pilate then asks the question that echoes down
the centuries—What is truth? (John 18:38). Finding
truth is the quest of life. Some respond instinctively
to the words of eternal life; others are less receptive.
All will have opportunity to hear the Savior's message
of truth and either embrace or reject his redeeming
love. Truth is not merely an abstract concept; it must
be applied to everyday living. Truth is reliable. Truth
is immutable and everlasting. All truth is circum-
scribed into one great whole, with Christ as the center.

Pilate answered them, saying, Will ye that I release unto you the King of the Jews? For he knew that the chief priests had delivered him for envy. But the chief priests moved the people, that he should rather release Barabbas unto them.

—MARK 15:9–11

The moment is filled with tragedy and dripping with irony. The people are about to put to death their long-awaited Messiah and King! Rather than release the Son of God the Father, they insist that the Romans release Barabbas, whose name means literally "son of the father." The gift had been proffered but refused. Jesus "so loved the world that he gave his own life, that as many as would believe might become the sons [and daughters] of God" (D&C 34:3). "For what doth it profit a man if a gift is bestowed upon him, and he receive not the gift? Behold, he rejoices not in that which is given unto him, neither rejoices in him who is the giver of the gift" (D&C 88:33).

Then Pilate therefore took Jesus, and scourged him.
—JOHN 19:1

Abinadi prophesied that Jesus would allow himself to be mocked, scourged, cast out, and disowned by his people (Mosiah 15:5). The unrelenting verbal abuse of Christ was quickly accompanied by harsh physical punishment to be culminated as Jesus was "led, crucified, and slain" for the sins of the world (Mosiah 15:7). Abinadi, who would himself endure scourging just before his death by fire, spoke by the spirit of prophecy as he told of the Son of God gaining ultimate victory over death. Scourging was preliminary to crucifixion, a vicious practice that assaulted both body and spirit. Abinadi was a type or shadow of the Savior to come. How fitting that this faithful messenger sealed the truth of his words by witnessing of Christ. Brutal scourging would dissuade neither Christ nor Abinadi from fulfilling their appointed missions.

SEPTEMBER

*Peace I leave with you, my peace I
give unto you: not as the world giveth,
give I unto you. Let not your heart be
troubled, neither let it be afraid.*

—JOHN 14:27

[Pilate] took water, and washed his hands before the multitude,
saying, I am innocent of the blood of this just person:
see ye to it. Then answered all the people, and said,
His blood be on us, and on our children.

—MATTHEW 27:24–25

Pilate followed the Jewish practice of performing a ceremonial hand washing to absolve himself of responsibility for Jesus' death (Deuteronomy 21:1–9). But he could never be fully free from culpability; his name is forever linked with the crucifixion of Christ. Pilate's lack of moral courage and his accountability for the suffering of Jesus pale in comparison, however, to the bloodthirsty cries of the crowd who demanded the death of Christ. Some five hundred years earlier, the Nephite prophet Jacob prophesied, "After they have hardened their hearts and stiffened their necks against the Holy One of Israel, behold the judgments of the Holy One of Israel shall come upon them. And the day cometh that they shall be smitten and afflicted" (2 Nephi 6:10). We cannot spurn the Light without opening ourselves to a life of darkness.

*And he bearing his cross went forth into a place called the place of
a burial, which is called in the Hebrew Golgotha;
where they crucified him, and two others with him,
on either side one, and Jesus in the midst.*
—JST JOHN 19:17–18

Crucifixion was a hideous and ignominious death. An evidence of the art of torture perfected by the Romans, it was also a method of execution to which the outcasts of Jewish society were consigned, for ancient law decreed: "If a man have committed a sin worthy of death, . . . and thou hang him on a tree: His body shall not remain all night upon the tree, but thou shalt in any wise bury him that day . . . that thy land be not defiled" (Deuteronomy 21:22–23) Thus the sinless Son of Man, he who had always conducted his life with dignity, was forced to endure the indignity of the lowest form of execution in dying between two thieves and making his grave with the wicked (Isaiah 53:9). "Though he was rich, yet for your sakes he became poor, that ye through his poverty might be rich" (2 Corinthians 8:9).

Then said the chief priests of the Jews to Pilate, Write not,
The King of the Jews; but that he said, I am King of the Jews.
Pilate answered, What I have written, I have written.
—JOHN 19:21–22

The Omniscient One moves in mysterious ways. He works his miracles in a fashion that we mortals would not have supposed. He speaks his decrees through the mouths of Nebuchadnezzar the Babylonian and Cyrus the Persian. Caiaphas, the pernicious and conniving high priest, surely did not grasp the full significance of his words when he said to the leaders of the Jews: "Ye know nothing at all, nor consider that it is expedient for us, that one man should die for the people, and that the whole nation perish not" (John 11:49–50). And finally there was Pontius Pilate, one of the most bloodthirsty and malicious leaders in Judea's history, refusing to yield to the entreaties of Jewish leaders to remove what he had written concerning Jesus of Nazareth—the blessed Messiah, the King of the Jews, the only and true King of the world.

*Then said Jesus, Father, forgive them; for they know not what
they do. And they parted his raiment, and cast lots.*
—LUKE 23:34

Joseph Smith's translation of the Bible informs us the
Lord prayed for the soldiers who crucified him. He
said, in effect, "'Father, lay not this sin to their charge,
for they are acting under orders, and those upon
whom the full and real guilt rests are their rulers and
the Jewish conspirators who caused me to be condemned. It is Caiaphas and Pilate who know I am
innocent; these soldiers are just carrying out their
orders'" (McConkie, *Doctrinal New Testament Commentary*, 1:818–19). Jesus asked forgiveness—but not for
the blameworthy. Mercy cannot rob justice; the guilty
cannot go free. Spoken by David more than a thousand years before, the messianic prophecy was here
fulfilled by Roman soldiers: "They part my garments
among them, and cast lots upon my vesture" (Psalm
22:18).

*And he said unto Jesus, Lord, remember me when thou comest
into thy kingdom. And Jesus said unto him, Verily I say
unto thee, To day shalt thou be with me in paradise.*
—LUKE 23:42–43

Although "all are within the reach of pardoning mercy" only he who keeps the commandments of our God will be saved (Smith, *Teachings of the Prophet Joseph Smith,* 191; Matthew 7:21–22). Did the Master actually promise the thief on the cross that he would enter paradise, the abode of the righteous? Would all his sins be overlooked? Joseph Smith stated: "There has been much said by modern divines about the words of Jesus . . . 'This day shalt thou be with me in paradise.' King James' translators make it out to say paradise. But what is paradise? It is a modern word: it does not answer at all to the original word that Jesus made use of. . . . There is nothing in the original word in Greek from which this was taken that signifies paradise; but it was—'This day thou shalt be with me in the world of spirits'" (*Teachings of the Prophet Joseph Smith,* 309).

When Jesus therefore saw his mother, and the disciple standing
by, whom he loved, he saith unto his mother, Woman, behold thy
son! Then saith he to the disciple, Behold thy mother!
And from that hour that disciple took her unto his own home.
—JOHN 19:26–27

Among the witnesses to Jesus Christ's crucifixion were those who watched in love and sorrow. During these hours of intense suffering, the Savior's solicitude turned to his dear mother, whose soul the sword had pierced, even as Simeon had prophesied at the temple (Luke 2:35). Mary, who had spoken with the angel Gabriel, given birth to God's Son, nurtured him, witnessed his mortal sojourn, and finally seen him crucified by evil men, needed support in her grief and help in her advancing years. Jesus had compassion for his mother and knew that he could trust John to care for her most tenderly. John led the mother of the Son of God away to his own home. Ever after, John honored this sacred stewardship and gave Mary a special place in his household.

*And when the sixth hour was come,
there was darkness over the whole land until the ninth hour.*
—MARK 15:33

Our Lord was placed upon the cross at the third hour, about nine o'clock in the morning, and he ministered from the cross for three hours. There the work of atonement continued, and all of the agonies of Gethsemane—the sufferings in body and spirit, the feelings of alienation and grief—resumed for another three hours on Golgotha. What had begun in the garden was now consummated on the cross. And the physical darkness that spread to all parts of the natural world attested to the spiritual darkness into which the Lord of the living and the dead was now descending. Zenos, the prophet of the brass plates, had testified centuries earlier: "And because of the groanings of the earth, many of the kings of the isles of the sea shall be wrought upon by the Spirit of God, to exclaim: The God of nature suffers" (1 Nephi 19:12).

And about the ninth hour Jesus cried with a loud voice,
saying, Eli, Eli, lama sabachthani? that is to say,
My God, my God, why hast thou forsaken me?
—MATTHEW 27:46

Matthew recorded that Jesus uttered a soul cry none of us can comprehend. He had never known the feelings of remorse or the pain of alienation from God that characterize the whole of humankind. Only Jesus could say: "My Father worketh hitherto, and I work" (John 5:17). "The Son can do nothing of himself, but what he seeth the Father do" (John 5:19). "My doctrine is not mine, but his that sent me" (John 7:16). "I and my Father are one" (John 10:30). "The Father hath not left me alone; for I do always those things that please him" (John 8:29). How utterly incapable then are we to fathom the infinite turmoil manifest in his beseeching, "My God, my God, why hast thou forsaken me?" When one has drawn close to the Father and enjoyed sweet communion through his Spirit, it is ever so much more painful to be separated.

*Jesus when he had cried again with a loud voice, saying,
Father, it is finished, thy will is done, yielded up the ghost.*
—JST MATTHEW 27:54

The hour had come; Jesus' mortal mission was complete. In accord with the Father's will, Jesus had given himself in atonement for the sins of the world and provided a rescue from spiritual and temporal death. Perfectly submissive, the Savior of the world fulfilled his earthly calling with exactness. The vital distinction between being slain and giving oneself voluntarily to death gives power and meaning to his sacrifice. Jesus could have chosen to live. He could have called down legions of heavenly hosts to rescue him, enacting justice upon his merciless persecutors. Instead, with supreme mercy, he saw it through to the end. He willingly "yielded up" his spirit: "I lay down my life. . . . No man taketh it from me, but I lay it down of myself" (John 10:17–18). This part of the plan was now ended, a perfect finish for a perfect life.

He said, Father, into thy hands I commend my spirit:
and having said thus, he gave up the ghost.
Now when the centurion saw what was done, he glorified God,
saying, Certainly this was a righteous man.
—LUKE 23:46–47

The Roman centurion and the soldiers under his command at the place of execution were amazed and greatly affrighted," wrote Elder James E. Talmage. "They had probably witnessed many deaths on the cross, but never before had they seen a man apparently die of his own volition, and able to cry in a loud voice at the moment of dissolution. That barbarous and inhuman mode of execution induced slow and progressive exhaustion. The actual death of Jesus appeared to all who were present to be a miracle, as in fact it was" (*Jesus the Christ,* 662–63). Jesus' regal demeanor as he gave up his life, accompanied with the earthquake and the rending of the rocks, so astonished the centurion and others that they solemnly declared, as other Gospel writers record, "Truly this was the Son of God" (Matthew 27:54; Mark 15:39).

And, behold, the veil of the temple was rent in twain from the top to the bottom; and the earth did quake, and the rocks rent.
—MATTHEW 27:51

From the days of Moses onward, the tabernacle in the wilderness contained a linen veil separating the two compartments known as the holy place and the holy of holies. The holiest of all places could be entered on only one day of the year, the Day of Atonement, and only by one man, the high priest. There he sprinkled blood upon the altar and called upon Jehovah for mercy in behalf of the nation of Israel. Now the great and last sacrifice had been offered and mercy extended through the blood of the Lamb of God. The law of Moses had come to an end, for it had been fulfilled in Christ. Like the flesh of Christ which was torn for our sins (Hebrews 10:20), the veil was rent in twain as entrance to the holiest of all places, the celestial kingdom, was made available to us.

But when they came to Jesus, and saw that he was dead already,
they brake not his legs: but one of the soldiers with a spear pierced
his side, and forthwith came there out blood and water.
—JOHN 19:33–34

Breaking the legs of those crucified often hastened
their death. But when the crucifiers came to Jesus,
they discovered that death had already come to him.
Thus was fulfilled the messianic word: "He keepeth all
his bones: not one of them is broken" (Psalm 34:20).
Also fulfilled was the prophecy of Zechariah: "I will
pour upon the house of David, and upon the inhabitants of Jerusalem, the spirit of grace and of supplications: and they shall look upon me whom they have
pierced, and they shall mourn for him, as one mour-
neth for his only son" (Zechariah 12:10). Mary, the
mother of Jesus, must have reflected painfully upon
the prophetic words spoken by Simeon more than
three decades earlier: "Yea, a spear shall pierce through
him to the wounding of thine own soul also; that the
thoughts of many hearts may be revealed" (JST
Luke 2:35).

This man went unto Pilate, and begged the body of Jesus.
And he took it down, and wrapped it in linen, and
laid it in a sepulchre that was hewn in stone,
wherein never man before was laid.
—LUKE 23:52—53

J oseph of Arimathea was a rich man of some influence in the community, and he was a disciple of Jesus who "waited for the kingdom of God" (Luke 23:51). He owned a new tomb hewn from the rock in a garden not far from Calvary. John records, "Now in the place where he was crucified there was a garden; and in the garden a new sepulchre, wherein was never man yet laid" (John 19:41). How fitting that this unused tomb would serve as sepulchre for the Son of God, the Unblemished Lamb, the Sinless One. The Rock of our salvation would break the bands of death and rise triumphant from this sepulchre hewn of rock.

Then she runneth, and cometh to Simon Peter, and to the other
disciple, whom Jesus loved, and saith unto them,
They have taken away the Lord out of the sepulchre,
and we know not where they have laid him.

—JOHN 20:2

Two angels of the Lord had rolled back the stone from the door of the tomb where Jesus' body was laid (JST Matthew 28:2–3). When Mary of Magdala saw it, she ran to tell the apostles. Like others, Mary feared that wicked men must have stolen the body of her Lord. Soon, however, the knowledge and witness of the literal resurrection of Jesus would come to Mary and to the apostles. They were about to discover that the empty tomb was the fulfillment of prophetic utterances through the ages: Christ the Lord had risen! After the ascension of the resurrected Lord, Jesus' followers designated Sunday as the day of worship to commemorate the day Jesus rose from the grave into everlasting life. This change was clearly pleasing to the Lord, who, in revelation to the Prophet Joseph Smith, referred to Sunday as "my holy day" (D&C 59:9).

*And they remembered his words, and returned from the sepulchre,
and told all these things unto the eleven, and to all the rest.*
—LUKE 24:8–9

Most of us are very much like the disciples of Jesus. Our leaders repeatedly teach sacred truths and bear testimony of important matters, and yet sometimes these things do not seem to penetrate our hearts. Then suddenly the light comes on, and we understand. So it was in the meridian of time. Jesus had spoken at length of his death and resurrection, of the redemption to be wrought by his rise from the tomb, but the idea seemed unfathomable to his disciples. And then it happened. He rose from the dead, he appeared and taught his own, and his hard sayings began to penetrate their softened hearts. They comprehended how it all fit into place in the Father's grand plan of salvation. Now Jesus' words, some of them spoken three years earlier, made perfect sense.

Why seek ye the living among the dead? He is not here,
but is risen: remember how he spake unto you
when he was yet in Galilee.
—LUKE 24:5–6

At times it is difficult to believe that the harsh reality of death holds the promise of resurrection. President Gordon B. Hinckley wrote these words while attending the funeral service of a friend:

> *What is this thing that men call death,*
> *This quiet passing in the night?*
> *'Tis not the end, but genesis*
> *Of better worlds and greater light.*
> *O God, touch Thou my aching heart,*
> *And calm my troubled, haunting fears.*
> *Let hope and faith, transcendent, pure,*
> *Give strength and peace beyond my tears.*
> *There is no death, but only change*
> *With recompense for victory won;*
> *The gift of Him who loved all men,*
> *The Son of God, the Holy One.*
> (Teachings of Gordon B. Hinckley, 552)

Christ is risen! and because he lives, we shall live also.

And the graves were opened; and many bodies of the saints which slept arose, and came out of the graves after his resurrection, and went into the holy city, and appeared unto many.
—MATTHEW 27:52–53

Jesus' rise from the tomb initiated the first resurrection, the resurrection of the righteous dead from the days of Adam to the Savior's ministry. This phenomenal experience, which occurred in the New World as well (Helaman 14:25; 3 Nephi 23:9–10), must have been both sobering and faith-building for the Saints. It affirmed all that the Master had spoken concerning the resurrection and thus confirmed their hope for the immortality of the soul and of an eventual reunion with departed loved ones. It is an experience that will be had again by those who are alive at the time of the Savior's return in glory, for "if we believe that Jesus died and rose again, even so them also which sleep in Jesus will God bring with him" (1 Thessalonians 4:14).

*And it came to pass, that, while they communed together and
reasoned, Jesus himself drew near, and went with them.
But their eyes were holden that they should not know him.*
—LUKE 24:15–16

We live in this world almost unaware that just
beyond the veil are those who love us and minister in
our behalf. When he was sustained as eleventh president of the Church, President Harold B. Lee said:
"There has been here an overwhelming spiritual
endowment, attesting, no doubt, that in all likelihood
we are in the presence of personages, seen and unseen,
who are in attendance. Who knows but that even our
Lord and Master would be near us on such an occasion as this, for we, and the world, must never forget
that this is his church, and under his almighty direction we are to serve! . . . The Lord said: 'Behold, verily, verily, I say unto you that mine eyes are upon you. I
am in your midst and ye cannot see me.' (D&C 38:7)"
(Conference Report, October 1972, 18).

*And they said one to another, Did not our heart burn
within us, while he talked with us by the way,
and while he opened to us the scriptures?*
—LUKE 24:32

What must it have been like to walk with and be
taught by the Master Teacher? While traveling with
the two disciples on the road to Emmaus, Jesus began
to place the events of the last week—the week of
atonement—into the grand perspective of the Father's
plan of salvation. "And beginning at Moses and all the
prophets, he expounded unto them in all the scriptures the things concerning himself" (Luke 24:27).
This episode provides a marvelous pattern for those
of us who aspire to teach the gospel with power and
persuasion. It motivates us to teach as he taught—to
search the revelations, to expound "all the scriptures
in one" (3 Nephi 23:14), and to do so in such a way
that the word of truth goes down into the hearts of
our listeners and burns like fire. This kind of teaching
brings conviction. It leads to lasting conversion.

*The same day . . . came Jesus and stood in the midst,
and saith unto them, Peace be unto you. And when he had so said,
he shewed unto them his hands and his side.
Then were the disciples glad.*

—JOHN 20:19 20

The Savior appeared to his startled disciples and continued teaching about the resurrection by showing them what a resurrected body was. Elder Bruce R. McConkie noted: "As Jesus stood before them he seemed in every respect to be a man. . . . He announced that his body was made of 'flesh and bones' and invited all present to handle, feel, and learn of its corporeal nature. Then lest any feel later that their senses had been deceived, he asked for food and ate it before them, not to satisfy hunger, but to demonstrate that resurrected beings are tangible and can eat and digest food" (*Doctrinal New Testament Commentary,* 1:852–53). The knowledge that "the Father has a body of flesh and bones as tangible as man's; the Son also" (D&C 130:22) brings us understanding and should affect our perspective on the physical body. Body and spirit, inseparable joined as the soul of man, will receive a fulness of joy (D&C 88:15; 93:33).

Peace be unto you. . . . Behold my hands and my feet,
that it is I myself: handle me, and see; for a spirit
hath not flesh and bones, as ye see me have.
—LUKE 24:36–39

Our faith as Christians is founded upon the belief that Jesus of Nazareth died, was buried, and rose again the third day. A belief in an actual, literal resurrection from the dead is, in fact, what Christianity is all about. Jesus was a great teacher, but others have taught profound truths. He was compassionate and caring, but others have looked to the welfare of their fellows. Jesus did what no other teacher or adviser or social revolutionary could do—he suffered and died for our sins, and he came back to life. The resurrection stands as the physical evidence that Jesus was indeed the Christ, the divine Redeemer, the promised Messiah.

Thomas answered and said unto him, My Lord and my
God. Jesus saith unto him, Thomas, because thou
hast seen me, thou hast believed: blessed are they
that have not seen, and yet have believed.
—JOHN 20:28–29

Thomas was not with the other disciples when they had seen Jesus. Rashly he said, "I'll believe when I see." Hence the oft-repeated phrase, "seeing is believing." But the Lord teaches a higher law: believing is seeing, for those who manifest faith will see even greater things; those who believe and have not seen are blessed (John 1:50; D&C 34:4). Seeing does not necessarily cement our faith in the Lord. There is a stronger manifestation than sight, and that is the witness of the Holy Ghost, who whispers peace to the soul and delivers light and knowledge to the mind. Strong faith most often does not come from a burning bush or a heavenly messenger. Deep faithfulness is born of the quiet whisperings of the Spirit. As we seek the Lord daily, our hearts are changed, and we truly begin to see.

Simon Peter saith unto them, I go a fishing. They say unto him,
We also go with thee. They went forth, and entered into a ship
immediately; and that night they caught nothing.

—JOHN 21:3

Not yet having received their great commission to bear witness to the world of the risen Lord, the disciples went back to work at their old jobs. Perhaps this earthly endeavor gave them opportunity to more fully ponder the things of heaven. It may be that they needed to meditate, to sort things out in their minds, and, being fishermen, they turned to the work in which they found confidence and security. All the world had been turned upside down. What would become of them? What would they do? Being reminded of everlasting things, these erstwhile fishermen caught nothing in their nets. The things of the world will never fully satisfy the soul. Only the Bread of Life brings "peace in this world, and eternal life in the world to come" (D&C 59:23).

*And he said unto them, Cast the net on the right side of the ship,
and ye shall find. They cast therefore, and now they were
not able to draw it for the multitude of fishes.*
—JOHN 21:6

The work of sharing the gospel is the Lord's work, and we must do it in his way or we will not succeed (D&C 49:4). Elder Dallin H. Oaks reminded us how vital it is that we have "divine assistance to guide us in sharing the gospel. Just as our desires must be pure and rooted in testimony and love, our actions must be directed by the Lord. It is His work, not ours, and it must be done in His way and on His timing, not ours. . . . The Lord loves all of His children. He desires that all have the fulness of His truth and the abundance of His blessings. He knows when they are ready, and He wants us to hear and heed His directions on sharing His gospel" (Conference Report, October 2001, 7). When we go forth to share the gospel as the Savior directs, the results will be glorious.

So when they had dined, Jesus saith to Simon Peter, Simon,
son of Jonas, lovest thou me more than these?
He saith unto him, Yea, Lord; thou knowest that
I love thee. He saith unto him, Feed my lambs.
—JOHN 21:15

Jesus essentially asked Peter, "Simon, do you love me more than you love these fish? Do you love me more than your previous way of life? If you do, then do as I have instructed you—see to the needs of your brothers and sisters. Teach the gospel. Build up and fortify the Saints." In like manner, the same Lord asks of us, "Do you love me more than your employment, more than your standing in the community? If so, then feed my sheep—love your family, teach and nurture them; serve faithfully in the Church; consecrate your time and talents and resources to my service; and keep yourselves unspotted from the sins of the world." If we truly love the Lord Jesus, we put him first and foremost in our lives. We do all in our power to build up the kingdom of God and establish Zion.

Then went this saying abroad among the brethren, that
that disciple should not die: yet Jesus said not unto
him, He shall not die; but, If I will that he
tarry till I come, what is that to thee?
—JOHN 21:23

When Peter learned of his future martyrdom (John 21:18–19), he desired to know what awaited his fellow apostle John the Beloved. Jesus had said earlier, "There be some standing here, which shall not taste of death, till they see the Son of man coming in his kingdom" (Matthew 16:28). The answer Jesus gave was that John would tarry in the flesh until Jesus returned in glory. John and the three Nephite disciples were translated, meaning they underwent a change in their bodies so they would not die. When the Lord returns, they will "be changed in the twinkling of an eye from mortality to immortality," and thus they "shall never taste of death" (3 Nephi 28:7–8; D&C 7).

Then the eleven disciples went away into Galilee, into a mountain
where Jesus had appointed them. And when they saw him,
they worshipped him: but some doubted.
—MATTHEW 28:16–17

Jesus promised his disciples on the night of his
betrayal and arrest: "After I am risen again, I will go
before you into Galilee" (Matthew 26:32). The angels
at the tomb commanded the women to tell his disciples: "He goeth before you into Galilee; there shall
ye see him" (Matthew 28:7; Mark 16:7). The biblical
account of this promised meeting is very brief, but it
was "likely the occasion of which, as Paul wrote later,
'he was seen of above five hundred brethren at once.'
(1 Cor. 15:6.) . . . We may suppose that great preparation preceded this meeting; that it dealt with many
things, perhaps being similar to his resurrected ministry to multitudes of Nephites; and that from it, by
the mouths of many witnesses, the sure testimony
of his divine Sonship went forth to the world"
(McConkie, *Doctrinal New Testament Commentary*,
1:866–67).

Go ye therefore, and teach all nations, baptizing them in the
name of the Father, and of the Son, and of the Holy Ghost:
Teaching them to observe all things whatsoever
I have commanded you.
—MATTHEW 28:19‑20

Apostles are called to be special witnesses of Christ
in all the world (Acts 1:22; D&C 107:23). They are to
testify of the divinity of the Savior, his atoning sacrifice, and his resurrection from the dead. Holding the
keys of the priesthood, they are called to be teachers
of truth, preachers of righteousness, and proclaimers
of Christ. Above all, they are sent forth to represent
the Lord at all times and in all places. Having entered
the gospel covenant, we too are called to be witnesses
for Christ (Moroni 4:3; 5:2). We do not need apostolic
keys to testify of Christ and stand as witnesses of him
at all times (Mosiah 18:9). We manifest Christ by the
way we live, the way we treat others, and the integrity
of our hearts. We reflect Jesus in our lives by doing our
best to follow him.

And these signs shall follow them that believe; in my name shall
they cast out devils; they shall speak with new tongues; . . .
they shall lay hands on the sick, and they shall recover.
—MARK 16:17–18

The Lord instructed the early Latter-day Saints that "faith cometh not by signs, but signs follow those that believe" (D&C 63:9). The signs of the Lord's true Church are the miracles and gifts and wonders that always accompany faith. They are evidences that the Spirit of God and the powers of the priesthood are operative among the people of the covenant. Moroni taught that any person who denies the need for such gifts "knoweth not the gospel of Christ; yea, he has not read the scriptures; if so, he does not understand them," for our God is "a God of miracles, . . . and it is that same God who created the heavens and the earth, and all things that in them are" (Mormon 9:8–11).

*But these [signs] are written, that ye might believe that
Jesus is the Christ, the Son of God; and that believing
ye might have life through his name.*
—JOHN 20:31

All scripture is written to persuade people that
Jesus is the Son of the living God. Nephi wrote, "And
we talk of Christ, we rejoice in Christ, we preach of
Christ, we prophesy of Christ, and we write according
to our prophecies, that our children may know to what
source they may look for a remission of their sins" (2
Nephi 25:26). President Gordon B. Hinckley, a modern special witness of Christ, has said, "He is the
Savior and the Redeemer of the world. I believe in
Him. I declare His divinity without equivocation or
compromise. I love Him. I speak His name in reverence and wonder. I worship Him as I worship His
Father, in spirit and in truth. I thank Him and kneel
before His wounded feet and hands and side, amazed
at the love He offers me" (*Teachings of Gordon B. Hinckley,*
276–77).

OCTOBER

*And as many as touched were
made perfectly whole.*
—MATTHEW 14:36

*Wherefore of these men which have companied with us all the
time that the Lord Jesus went in and out among us, . . . unto
that same day that he was taken up from us, must one be
ordained to be a witness with us of his resurrection.*
—ACTS 1:21–22

President Harold B. Lee told of two missionaries
who had "what seemed to them a very difficult question. A young Methodist minister had laughed at them
when they had said that apostles were necessary today
in order for the true church to be upon the earth. . . . I
said to them, 'Go back and ask your minister friend
two questions. First, how did the Apostle Paul gain
what was necessary to be called an apostle? He didn't
know the Lord, had no personal acquaintance. . . . And
the second question you ask him is, How does he
know that all who are today apostles have not likewise
received that witness?' I bear witness to you that those
who hold the apostolic calling may, and do, know of
the reality of the mission of the Lord. To know is to be
born and quickened in the inner man" (*Stand Ye in Holy
Places,* 64–65).

There came a sound from heaven as of a rushing mighty wind, . . .
And they were all filled with the Holy Ghost, and began to
speak with other tongues, as the Spirit gave them utterance.
—ACTS 2:2–4

Pentecost was one of the major festivals of the
Israelites, one that came some fifty days after Passover.
It was the feast of first fruits, a time of celebration of
the Lord's outpouring of goodness and grace. Now, in
compliance with the words of Jesus before his final
ascent, the "promise of the Father" had been given: the
Holy Spirit was poured out in a powerful manner, and
the people were endowed with power from on high.
In both the Hebrew and Greek languages, the word
translated "spirit" can also be translated as "breath" or
"wind." Thus a great wind was felt by the people, sym-
bolizing a mighty endowment of the Spirit of God.

Then Peter said unto them, Repent, and be baptized every one of you in the name of Jesus Christ for the remission of sins, and ye shall receive the gift of the Holy Ghost.
—ACTS 2:38

As the Lord's senior apostle, Peter knew the requirements for salvation. He knew it was not enough to merely confess the name of Jesus, live a moral life, and believe that all roads lead to heaven. In response to the question "What shall we do?" Peter taught the first principles and ordinances of the gospel. These are outlined so clearly for us in the fourth Article of Faith: "first, Faith in the Lord Jesus Christ; second, Repentance; third, Baptism by immersion for the remission of sins; fourth, Laying on of hands for the gift of the Holy Ghost." The first four principles and ordinances of the gospel open the way for salvation in the kingdom of God.

Peter said, Silver and gold have I none; but such as I have give I thee: In the name of Jesus Christ of Nazareth rise up and walk. And he took him by the right hand, and lifted him up.
—ACTS 3:6–7

To the lame man asking for alms, Peter offers a treasure of inestimable worth. The man exercises faith in the Lord, and Peter heals him. Though lame from birth, the man rose to his feet and walked. Acting in the Lord's name and by the authority of the holy priesthood which he held, Peter pronounced the miracle. He had witnessed the Savior heal the lame. He had been tutored by the Lord and now followed his example. In the words of President Harold B. Lee, "You cannot lift another soul until you are standing on higher ground that he is. You must be sure, if you would rescue the man, that you yourself are setting the example of what you would have him be. You cannot light a fire in another soul unless it is burning in your own soul" (Conference Report, April 1973, 178).

*He shall send Jesus Christ, . . . whom the heaven must receive
until the times of restitution of all things, which God hath spoken
by the mouth of all his holy prophets since the world began.*
—ACTS 3:20–21

Peter spoke prophetically of the times of the restitution of all things, the era in which God would make all things right by restoring all things true—this is our day. It is a day long foreseen by prophets, a day in which sacred powers and principles and doctrines would be made known "which our forefathers have awaited with anxious expectation to be revealed in the last times, which their minds were pointed to by the angels" (D&C 121:27). We rejoice that

> *The morning breaks, the shadows flee;*
> *Lo, Zion's standard is unfurled!*
> *The dawning of a brighter day,*
> *Majestic rises on the world.*
>
> (Hymns, *no. 1*)

Neither is there salvation in any other: for there is none other name under heaven given among men, whereby we must be saved.
—ACTS 4:12

Salvation is in Christ and no other. As the Only Begotten of the Father, the literal Son of God, he is the Anointed One, the only person born into the world with the power to work out the infinite atonement. He is the Resurrection and the Life, our Savior and Redeemer, the Light of the world. Were it not for his loving redemption, all of us would be lost forever (2 Nephi 9:6–9). This same truth was spoken by King Benjamin many decades before the birth of Christ: "There shall be no other name given nor any other way nor means whereby salvation can come unto the children of men, only in and through the name of Christ, the Lord Omnipotent" (Mosiah 3:17).

A certain man named Ananias, with Sapphira his wife,
sold a possession, and kept back part of the price,
his wife also being privy to it, and brought a certain
part, and laid it at the apostles' feet.

—ACTS 5:1–2

Ananias and Sapphira—and the Saints of their
day—learned a lesson long to be remembered. Having
voluntarily covenanted to consecrate all they had to
the Lord, they devised a plan: they "kept back" a portion of their property. But Simon Peter, moved upon
by that Spirit that searches hearts, confronted the
deceptive couple with the penetrating words: "Thou
hast not lied unto men, but unto God" (Acts 5:4).
Both Ananias and Sapphira, exposed in their
hypocrisy, fell dead at the feet of the apostles. This
story is harsh and dramatic. It is, however, symbolic of
the spiritual death that surely comes to all who follow
such a course. The issue, then, is one of trust. The
Almighty, who promises us all that he has, asks simply
that we be willing to give him all. Nothing less will do.

*Refrain from these men, and let them alone: for if this counsel
or this work be of men, it will come to naught: But if it
be of God, ye cannot overthrow it; lest haply ye
be found even to fight against God.*
—ACTS 5:38–39

Who of us wants to stand in the way of progress,
especially the progress of the kingdom of God? Who
among us desires to be numbered with the stumbling
blocks on the strait path of the Master? Jesus spoke of
how true and false prophets could be discerned: the
test of their fruits, what comes of their labors
(Matthew 7:15–16). Gamaliel's bit of counsel might
well be called the test of time. If a given work or teaching is not of God, it will eventually either dissolve
beneath the weight of its own irrelevance or begin to
manifest its own falsehood. Of the work of salvation,
the Master explained: "Verily, thus saith the Lord unto
you—there is no weapon that is formed against you
shall prosper; and if any man lift his voice against you
he shall be confounded in mine own due time" (D&C
71:9–10).

And the Lord said, I am Jesus whom thou persecutest: it is hard
for thee to kick against the pricks. And he trembling and
astonished said, Lord, what wilt thou have me to do?
—ACTS 9:5–6

Kicking against the pricks is a metaphor that refers
to how an ox hurts itself by fighting its master's prod.
It points to the wounds we inflict upon ourselves by
failing to follow divine direction. "Sooner or later each
of us must face God," said Elder Neal A. Maxwell. "Of
course, for all of us, now is the best time to serve the
Lord. And if you sense that one day every knee shall
bow and every tongue shall confess that Jesus Christ
is the Lord, why not do so now?" (Conference Report,
October 1974, 16). The Lord is grieved when we, like
Paul, fail to pay heed to the word of divine truth. He
stands ready to answer the question, "Lord, what wilt
thou have me to do?" if we will but ask.

Peter opened his mouth, and said, Of a truth I perceive that God is no respecter of persons: but in every nation he that feareth him, and worketh righteousness, is accepted with him.

—ACTS 10:34–35

Peter explains the full meaning of the Lord's decree, "Go ye into all the world, and preach the gospel to every creature" (Mark 16:15). By the spirit of revelation, he teaches the apostles that the gospel door should now be open to all nations, after many years in which the law had gone to Israel only. Peter affirms the resurrected Lord's will that all of his children, no matter their race or religion, have the opportunity of receiving the gospel. The great Nephite missionary Ammon taught, "God is mindful of every people, whatsoever land they may be in; yea, he numbereth his people, and his bowels of mercy are over all the earth" (Alma 26:37).

To him give all the prophets witness, that through his name whosoever believeth in him shall receive remission of sins.
—ACTS 10:43

The gospel message is always taught by witnesses. "In the mouth of two or three witnesses shall every word be established," wrote the apostle Paul (2 Corinthians 13:1). Witnesses are sent to testify of Christ, to call people to repentance, to declare the good tidings of the great plan of happiness and the way of eternal life. Salvation for all people in every age is found in Jesus Christ and in no other (Mosiah 4:7–8). From Adam to our day, preachers of righteousness proclaim the everlasting gospel covenant, a covenant centered in Christ. There is one system of salvation, one focal point of the teachings of all prophets, seers, and revelators. It is in him, the Son of God, the Savior and Redeemer of all.

*God . . . hath made of one blood all nations of men for to dwell on
all the face of the earth, and hath determined the times before
appointed, and the bounds of their habitation.*
—Acts 17:24–26

Birth and life and death are part of God's great plan
of happiness, and nothing is left to chance. Moses
explained: "When the most High divided to the
nations their inheritance, when he separated the sons
of Adam, he set the bounds of the people according to
the number of the children of Israel. For the Lord's
portion is his people; Jacob is the lot of his inheritance" (Deuteronomy 32:8–9). President Harold B.
Lee declared: "You are now born into a family to
which you have come, into the nations through which
you have come, as a reward for the kind of lives you
lived before you came here and at a time in the world's
history . . . determined by the faithfulness of each of
those who lived before this world was created"
(Conference Report, October 1973, 7).

So worship I the God of my fathers, believing all things which are written in the law and in the prophets: and have hope toward God . . . that there shall be a resurrection of the dead.
—ACTS 24:14–15

All scripture testifies of Christ and the great gospel plan. Prophets and witnesses of Christ do the same: teach the doctrine and then testify by the power of the Spirit that it is true. Paul, in the great paradox of the committed Christian, is both humbly submissive and boldly confident in his missionary efforts. "There came many to him into his lodging; to whom he expounded and testified the kingdom of God, persuading them concerning Jesus, both out of the law of Moses, and out of the prophets, from morning till evening" (Acts 28:23). Paul spoke of his transforming experience, utilized the holy scriptures to testify of Christ, and bore witness of the truth found in Jesus. He summed it all up with a powerful mission statement: to have a conscience that is clear toward God and all people (compare D&C 135:4).

Then Agrippa said unto Paul, Almost thou persuadest me to be a
Christian. And Paul said, I would to God, that not only thou,
but also all that hear me this day, were both almost,
and altogether such as I am.
—ACTS 26:28–29

Those who are spiritually deaf cannot comprehend a humble testimony when they hear it. Even some with testimonies cannot fully commit to Christ because they are afraid to relinquish their way of life. Like Joseph Smith, Paul cared little for the things of this world. Both gave their lives for their testimonies. The Prophet Joseph wrote, "I have thought . . . that I felt much like Paul, when he made his defense before King Agrippa, and related the account of the vision he had when he saw a light, and heard a voice; but still there were but few who believed him; some said he was dishonest, others said he was mad; and he was ridiculed and reviled. But all this did not destroy the reality of his vision. . . . Why persecute me for telling the truth?" (Joseph Smith–History 1:24–25).

For I am not ashamed of the gospel of Christ: for it is the power of God unto salvation to every one that believeth.
—ROMANS 1:16

The psalmist declared, "I will speak of thy testimonies also before kings, and will not be ashamed" (Psalm 119:46). Whether in company with kings or common citizens, we need never be ashamed of the restored gospel. Courageously standing for truth is part of living the gospel. If we trust in God and keep his commandments, we can accomplish anything he asks us to do. Sharing the gospel with a feeling of quiet confidence and a spirit of serenity can be a joy and a blessing. President Gordon B. Hinckley has said, "This work is nothing of which we need be ashamed. It is something in which we can take great pride. The problem is that most of us are filled with fear. . . . Try it. Taste the sweet and wonderful joy of sharing your testimony of this work with others" (*Teachings of Gordon B. Hinckley,* 373–74).

For all have sinned, and come short of the glory of God;
Therefore being justified only by his grace through
the redemption that is in Christ Jesus.
—JST ROMANS 3:23–24

Noneof us can be justified by works alone because we are all sinners. How, then, can we be saved? What will free us from the stain of sin and leave us pure and spotless? Some intervening and compensating power must bridge the gap. That power is provided by the Savior, the only perfect person ever to walk the earth. He had no sin, lived the law flawlessly, and therefore never estranged himself from God. He gave his life to pay the debt of sin for all who believe on his name, repent, and come unto him with full purpose of heart. His amazing grace becomes the source of our justification with God. Through the enabling power of his blood, we gain redemption. The Lawgiver, not the law, brings salvation.

Therefore we are buried with him by baptism unto death: that like as Christ was raised up from the dead by the glory of the Father, even so we also should walk in newness of life.
—ROMANS 6:4

Life and death are defined in terms of one another. In a sense, we must die as pertaining to our first estate in order to be born into the second. We must die as pertaining to worldliness in order to be born again unto righteousness. And we must die physically in order to be born into immortality and eternal life. The great challenge of the man or woman who strives for spirituality is to put the old man or woman to death— to put off the natural man, put on Christ, and thereby become a Saint through the Atonement (Mosiah 3:19). Those who do so are not only cleansed and purified but also strengthened and empowered to "walk in the light, as [Christ] is in the light" (1 John 1:7). They have come alive. They have become new creatures in Christ.

*For the wages of sin is death; but the gift of God is
eternal life through Jesus Christ our Lord.*
—ROMANS 6:23

Paul explains that the only recompense for sin is spiritual death, whereas the greatest gift of God, received through righteous living, is everlasting life. Alma explains this principle well: "Every man receiveth wages of him whom he listeth to obey" (Alma 3:27). Later Alma teaches: "If ye are not the sheep of the good shepherd, of what fold are ye? Behold, I say unto you, that the devil is your shepherd, and ye are of his fold. . . . And whosoever doeth this must receive his wages of him; therefore, for his wages he receiveth death, as to things pertaining to righteousness, being dead unto all good works" (Alma 5:39–42). In short, Satan "pays" his followers with spiritual death; Jesus rewards those who sincerely follow him with eternal life in the presence of God.

For to be carnally minded is death; but to be spiritually minded is
life and peace. Because the carnal mind is enmity against God:
for it is not subject to the law of God, neither indeed can be.
—ROMANS 8:6–7

To be carnally minded means to have enmity or hostility toward God. It implies pride and hardness of heart, placing ourselves either above or below the commandments. King Benjamin teaches how to be more spiritually minded. He reminds us that the natural man is an enemy to God, and unless we yield to the Holy Spirit and become as a child, "submissive, meek, humble, patient, full of love" (Mosiah 3:19), we cannot be saved. Salvation requires a conscious turning away from the things of this world and seeking for the things of eternity. Moreover, abiding peace and newness of life come from turning our hearts to God. Those who love God and put off the natural man enjoy the fruit of the Spirit. They feel more of God's love, peace, and joy. The things of this world no longer satisfy, and they "look to God and live" (Alma 37:47).

The Spirit itself beareth witness with our spirit, that we are the
children of God: And if children, then heirs; heirs of God,
and joint-heirs with Christ; if so be that we suffer
with him, that we may be also glorified together.
—ROMANS 8:16–17

All human beings—male and female—are created
in the image of God. Each is a beloved spirit son or
daughter of heavenly parents, and, as such, each has a
divine nature and destiny" ("The Family: A Proclamation to the World," *Ensign,* November 1995, 102). Like
any loving parent, our Father in Heaven wants for us
all that he has. President Joseph Fielding Smith wrote:
"Those who receive exaltation in the celestial kingdom
are promised the fulness thereof. . . . Man has within
him the power, which the Father has bestowed upon
him, so to develop in truth, faith, wisdom, and all
the virtues, that eventually he shall become like the
Father and the Son, . . . possessing the same attributes
in their perfection" (*Selections from Doctrines of Salvation,*
526–27, 530).

*But the Spirit itself maketh intercession for us with groanings
which cannot be uttered. And he that searcheth the hearts
knoweth what is the mind of the Spirit, because he maketh
intercession for the saints according to the will of God.*
—ROMANS 8:26–27

So often we pray in terms of our wants, seldom to address our true needs. But "the Spirit searcheth all things, yea, the deep things of God" (1 Corinthians 2:10). There are things we feel deep down that need to be brought to the surface, things that we really ought to pray for. These matters can be known only by revelation as the Holy Spirit brings them into our conscious mind. If we are attentive and reverent in our prayers, there come those rare moments when we find our words reaching beyond our thoughts, pleading in behalf of persons and circumstances that we had not planned to pray for. The Lord has instructed the Saints in our dispensation: "And if ye are purified and cleansed from all sin, ye shall ask whatsoever you will in the name of Jesus and it shall be done" (D&C 50:29).

For I am persuaded, that neither death, nor life, nor angels,
nor principalities, nor powers, nor things present, nor things
to come, nor height, nor depth, nor any other creature,
shall be able to separate us from the love of God.
—ROMANS 8:38 39

Through the ages, prophets have extolled the love of God, the necessity of being "clasped in the arms of Jesus" (Mormon 5:11). Lehi proclaimed, "The Lord hath redeemed my soul from hell; and I have beheld his glory, and I am encircled about eternally in the arms of his love" (2 Nephi 1:15). Nephi wrote, "The love of God, which sheddeth itself abroad in the hearts of the children of men . . . is the most desirable above all things" (1 Nephi 11:22). King Benjamin taught, "If ye do this ye shall always rejoice, and be filled with the love of God, and always retain a remission of your sins" (Mosiah 4:12). John says it all, "In this was manifested the love of God toward us, because that God sent his only begotten Son into the world, that we might live through him" (1 John 4:9).

They are not all Israel, which are of Israel.
—ROMANS 9:6

It is important to know who we are and Whose we are. We are the sons and daughters of an Eternal Father, we have been created in his image, and we have the capacity to become like him. It is also important to know that we are the sons and daughters of Abraham, Isaac, and Jacob, that we are children of the covenant, lineal descendants of the fathers. And yet, salvation does not come to us automatically because of whose descendant we are; salvation comes through a choice to follow Christ. Nephi taught that "as many of the Gentiles as will repent are the covenant people of the Lord; and as many of the Jews as will not repent shall be cast off; for the Lord covenanteth with none save it be with them who repent and believe in his Son" (2 Nephi 30:2).

For they being ignorant of God's righteousness, and going about to establish their own righteousness, have not submitted themselves unto the righteousness of God. For Christ is the end of the law for righteousness to every one that believeth.

ROMANS 10:3 4

Like all true ministers of Christ, Paul wanted to save souls. But he knew that zeal without correct knowledge and understanding does not save. Even when sincere, belief in falsehood cannot lead to salvation. Seeking our own course or worshipping false gods (including the false god of self-aggrandizement) leads to dead ends of discouragement, despair, and deception. In our day, the fulness of salvation comes through the new and everlasting gospel covenant as revealed and administered through Joseph Smith and latter-day prophets. The law given to Israel has an end in Christ, and salvation is available for "all those who have a broken heart and a contrite spirit; and unto none else can the ends of the law be answered" (2 Nephi 2:7). Eternal life is in Jesus Christ and is obtainable only by those who humbly follow him.

Whosoever shall call upon the name of the Lord shall be saved.
How then shall they call on him in whom they have not believed?
and how shall they believe in him of whom they have not heard?
and how shall they hear without a preacher?
—ROMANS 10:13–14

We have a sacred duty to lift up our voices and declare the word of God and his restored gospel covenant to the world. To do so, we must have a knowledge of God, fully embrace the gospel of his Son, and live in conformity to its truths. No one can be saved in ignorance or in sin. We are to call upon God for deliverance and, by example, encourage others to do the same. King Benjamin expressed it thus: "Retain the name written always in your hearts, that ye are not found on the left hand of God, but that ye hear and know the voice by which ye shall be called. . . . For how knoweth a man the master whom he has not served, and who is a stranger unto him, and is far from the thoughts and intents of his heart?" (Mosiah 5:12–13).

Be not conformed to this world:
but be ye transformed by the renewing of your mind,
that ye may prove what is that good,
and acceptable, and perfect, will of God.
—ROMANS 12:2

As we make the supreme decision of life—to follow Christ and surrender our will to him—we open ourselves to the cleansing and empowering presence of the Spirit of God. By virtue of the blood of Jesus Christ and through the medium of the Holy Ghost, we are purified of worldliness and pride and are sanctified of all desires for sin. Further, our minds are transformed so that we see what we ought to see. The call is for us to "come unto Christ, who is the Holy One of Israel, and partake of his salvation, and the power of his redemption. Yea, come unto him, and offer your whole souls as an offering unto him, and continue in fasting and praying, and endure to the end; and as the Lord liveth ye will be saved" (Omni 1:26).

*Let every soul be subject unto the higher powers.
For there is no power in the church but of God;
the powers that be are ordained of God. . . . But first,
render to all their dues, according to custom.*
—JST ROMANS 13:1–7

The Joseph Smith Translation clarifies that Paul was not speaking of government authorities, as commonly supposed, but of the governing authorities in the Church. Part of the process of consecration is learning to surrender our will to God's and to follow the counsel of his servants. "To gain salvation the saints must be subject to God's ministers," wrote Elder Bruce R. McConkie. "The doctrines and ordinances of the gospel cannot be separated from those appointed to teach Christ's gospel and perform his ordinances. . . . The Lord's covenant or gospel is always administered by those whom he has appointed so to act, and as a consequence the saints are bound to take counsel and direction from them" (*Doctrinal New Testament Commentary,* 2:296).

*Not many wise men after the flesh, not many mighty, not many
noble, are called: but God hath chosen the foolish things of the
world to confound the wise; and God hath chosen the weak things
of the world to confound the things which are mighty.*
—I Corinthians 1:26–27

The Lord works through the weak and the simple to
accomplish his purposes. Too often those who are
wealthy, educated, or famous tend to trust in their own
native ability or in their notoriety to get things done.
But the Almighty, who is able to do his own work (2
Nephi 27:20), prefers to work through the humble,
the meek, the submissive among us. These are they
who know their limits, who acknowledge their weakness, and who therefore lean upon and trust in the
Infinite One. Truly, "the weak things of the world shall
come forth and break down the mighty and strong
ones, that [uninspired] man should not counsel his
fellow man, neither trust in the arm of flesh" (D&C
1:19).

It is written, Eye hath not seen, nor ear heard,
neither have entered into the heart of man, the things
which God hath prepared for them that love him.
—1 CORINTHIANS 2:9

The Prophet Joseph Smith said that "we never can comprehend the things of God and of heaven, but by revelation" (*Teachings of the Prophet Joseph Smith,* 292). Only by the power of the Holy Ghost can the fulness of gospel blessings be both understood and received. The Lord declared, "For by my Spirit will I enlighten them, and by my power will I make known unto them the secrets of my will—yea, even those things which eye has not seen, nor ear heard, nor yet entered into the heart of man" (D&C 76: 10). Revelation is for every faithful follower of the Lord who has entered the waters of baptism and then received the gift of the Holy Ghost. Our happiness in this life and in the world to come is closely related to how fully we cultivate the spirit of revelation.

*But the natural man receiveth not the things of the Spirit of God:
for they are foolishness unto him: neither can he know them,
because they are spiritually discerned.*
—I CORINTHIANS 2:14

We have been counseled to "seek learning, even by study and also by faith" (D&C 88:118). There are many things we come to know in this world through investigation. But there are some things—things withheld from the skeptic, the cynic, the doubter—that can be known only by the quiet whisperings of the Spirit of the living God. Saving truths such as the divine Sonship of Christ, the appearance of the Father and the Son in the Sacred Grove, the truthfulness of the Book of Mormon, the restoration of priesthood keys and powers, and the status of The Church of Jesus Christ of Latter-day Saints as "the only true and living church upon the face of the whole earth" (D&C 1:30) can only be known by personal revelation, as the God of heaven chooses to endow his children with understanding.

I have planted, Apollos watered; but God gave the increase.
—1 CORINTHIANS 3:6

So often one sows while another reaps. One set of faithful missionaries works their hardest and spreads the seeds of testimony far and wide, but no convert baptisms take place during their stay in the area. Months or years later, their successors come into town, revisit the investigators, bear witness anew, fan the flame that once burned, and see testimony ripen. While each ambassador of the faith brings a new set of talents and abilities, and perhaps even a more convincing witness of this work, it is the Lord, through his Spirit, that brings about true conversion. Men and women are but instruments in the hands of the Master. God calls them, empowers them, and guides their labors, and thus the honor and glory for the fruits that follow belong to him whose work this is.

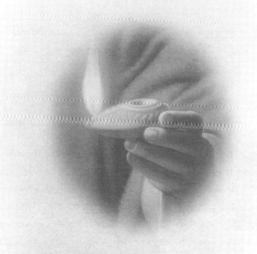

NOVEMBER

I am the light of the world:
he that followeth me shall not walk in
darkness, but shall have
the light of life.

—LUKE 8:12

Know ye not that ye are the temple of God, and that the
Spirit of God dwelleth in you? If any man defile the
temple of God, him shall God destroy; for the
temple of God is holy, which temple ye are.
—1 CORINTHIANS 3:16–17

Just as we would not trample the temple with muddy feet, so we must not allow the filth of immorality to walk through our souls. Our bodies are God-given and are meant to house the Spirit of the Lord. We are to keep them clean and modestly attired. We are expected to purify our hearts and keep them undefiled (D&C 133:5). Nothing threatens the purpose of marriage and family life as severely as infidelity does. Cleanliness in thought and action, so vital to one's spirituality and the well-being of the next generation, are abandoned in the moment of infidelity. We can build a strong link in a chain that ripples down the generations by remembering that we are the temples of God. To be clean is to be saved; to be filthy is to be damned.

Know ye not that your body is the temple of the
Holy Ghost which is in you, which ye have of God,
and ye are not your own? For ye are bought with a price.
—1 CORINTHIANS 6:19–20

In a world that is obsessed with freedom and crusades for "choice," Paul's words about our bodies may seem harsh. Indeed, the cry of our times that "my body is my own" is simply false. We are not our own. We have been bought with an infinite price—we have been bought "with the precious blood of Christ, as of a lamb without blemish and without spot" (1 Peter 1:19). We are a peculiar, that is, a *purchased* people: "For, behold, the Lord your Redeemer suffered death in the flesh; wherefore he suffered the pain of all men, that all men might repent and come unto him. And he hath risen again from the dead, that he might bring all men unto him, on conditions of repentance. And how great is his joy in the soul that repenteth!" (D&C 18:11–13).

Know ye not that they which run in a race run all,
but one receiveth the prize? So run, that ye may obtain.
—1 CORINTHIANS 9:24

The Apostle Paul spent much of his life teaching and encouraging spirituality in the then far-flung missions of the world," said Elder Howard W. Hunter. "He said that a Saint successfully keeping the commandments is like an athlete winning his contest; that comparable degrees of training, exertion, obedience to the rules, self-discipline, and the will to win are involved. To the Corinthians he wrote words which, paraphrased, are to this effect: 'You know (do you not?) that at the sports all the runners run the race, though only one wins the prize. Like them, run to win!'" (Conference Report, April 1979, 35). God is all-powerful, and in the end, the victory over death and hell will be his. Likewise, those who inherit the fulness of his glory are those who win the race of mortality and overcome all things.

God is faithful, who will not suffer you to be tempted above that ye are able; but will with the temptation also make a way to escape, that ye may be able to bear it.
—1 CORINTHIANS 10:13

The same Lord who parted the Red Sea so that Israel might escape bondage provides ways for us to escape temptation. The psalmist declared, "The righteous cry, and the Lord heareth, and delivereth them out of all their troubles" (Psalm 34:17). Customized challenges beset us all, but the Lord has promised us that with his divine help we can withstand every evil enticement and bear every affliction. The Lord's love and light is far more powerful than any of the adversary's lures. Satan cannot compel us to sin or tempt us beyond our ability to resist. Strength to shun temptation comes from the Lord through sincere prayer, scripture study, devotion to truth, and humble submission to his will. The more fully we give our hearts to God, the less room we'll have for temptation and sin.

Nevertheless neither is the man without the woman,
neither the woman without the man, in the Lord.
—1 CORINTHIANS 11:11

The roles of men and women in life are different but equally important. Some roles are better suited to the masculine nature; others require the natural and innate capacities of women. Men and women are entitled to every spiritual gift, every virtue, and every fruit of the Spirit. Priesthood is not maleness, nor should it be equated with male administration. Priesthood is divine authority given to worthy men as a part of God's great plan of happiness. The highest ordinances of the priesthood, received in the temple, are given only to a man and a woman together. Eternal life entails the continuation of the family unit, including the sanctified and ennobled union of a righteous man and a righteous woman, into the eternities.

*For as the body is one, and hath many members, and all the
members of that one body, being many, are one body: so also is
Christ. . . . For the body is not one member, but many.*
—I CORINTHIANS 12:12–14

Every man or woman who has been baptized and
has received the gift of the Holy Ghost has been given
at least one of the gifts of the Spirit (D&C 46:11). The
Church is called the body of Christ, and each member
makes a distinctive contribution to the spirituality of
the Saints and the blessing of the world. The whole is
so much stronger than the sum of the parts.
"Therefore, let every man stand in his own office, and
labor in his own calling; and let not the head say unto
the feet it hath no need of the feet; for without the
feet how shall the body be able to stand? Also the body
hath need of every member, that all may be edified
together, that the system may be kept perfect" (D&C
84:109–10).

Though I speak with the tongues of men and of angels, . . . and
though I have all faith, so that I could remove mountains,
and have not charity, I am nothing.
—1 CORINTHIANS 13:1–2

Nephi learned that the tree of life was a grand, eternal symbol of "the love of God, which sheddeth itself abroad in the hearts of the children of men" (1 Nephi 11:22). But this love of God was not just an abstract sentiment—it was manifest in the atoning gift of Jesus Christ (John 3:16). Charity, as Mormon taught, is "the pure love of Christ" (Moroni 7:47). It is "in the gift of his Son" that God has "prepared a more excellent way" and granted to us "a more excellent hope" (1 Corinthians 12:31; Ether 12:11, 32.) Having been cleansed and renewed by this love of God, we feel toward others a portion of what he feels toward us. "Beloved, if God so loved us, we ought also to love one another" (1 John 4:11).

If in this life only we have hope in Christ,
we are of all men most miserable.
—1 CORINTHIANS 15:19

Jesus Christ, the Hope of Israel, is the Redeemer not only of the living but also of the dead. "If it is for this life only that Christ has given us hope, we of all people are most to be pitied" (Revised English Bible, 1 Corinthians 15:19). His ministry spanned the veil of death, and his powerful effect upon humankind reaches into the eternities. The Prophet Joseph Smith taught: "If this life were all, we should be led to query, whether or not there was really any substance in existence, and we might with propriety say, 'Let us eat, drink, and be merry, for to-morrow we die!' . . . But this life is not all; the voice of *reason,* the language of *inspiration,* and the Spirit of the living God, our Creator, teaches us, as we hold the record of truth in our hands, that this is not the case" (*Teachings of the Prophet Joseph Smith,* 56).

*But now is Christ risen from the dead, and become the firstfruits
of them that slept. . . . For as in Adam all die,
even so in Christ shall all be made alive.*

—1 CORINTHIANS 15:20–22

Each of us, at one time or another, will have the difficult and dreaded opportunity to stand or kneel beside a loved one who is about to leave this life. Even those who rejoice in the liberating truths of the restored gospel may hesitate to let beloved parents or children or friends go. We are frightened by the separation and stricken by the break in loving associations. But he who orchestrates the events of our lives has made it known to us that death helps to fulfill "the merciful plan of the great Creator" (2 Nephi 9:6). The scriptures affirm and the Spirit attests the immortality of the soul, the reality of the resurrection, and the sweet reunion with loved ones in a future day. "Weeping may endure for a night," the psalmist wrote, "but joy cometh in the morning" (Psalm 30:5).

*Else what shall they do which are baptized for the dead,
if the dead rise not at all? why are they
then baptized for the dead?*

—I CORINTHIANS 15:29

Paul's reference to baptism for the dead in the context of the resurrection provides a significant window into the early Church, indicating to us that proxy baptisms were then being performed. Wrote Elder Bruce R. McConkie: "Obviously, during the frequent periods of apostate darkness when the gospel light does not shine, and also in those geographical areas where legal administrators are not found, hosts of people live and die without ever entering in at the gate of baptism so as to be on the path leading to eternal life. For them a just God has ordained baptism for the dead, a vicarious-proxy labor. Baptism for the dead is thus one of the signs of the true Church. Where a people have the knowledge of this doctrine, together with the power and authority from God to perform the saving ordinances involved, there is the Church and kingdom of God on earth" (*Doctrinal New Testament Commentary*, 2:395–96).

But some man will say, How are the dead raised up?
and with what body do they come?
—I CORINTHIANS 15:35

We will come forth from the grave with a resurrected body free of mortal imperfections (Alma 40:23). But though we will be refined, renewed, and perfected in the resurrection, we will maintain our identity. We will know friends and loved ones even as we know them now. Speaking of meeting a departed loved one after death, President Joseph F. Smith taught: "I expect to be able to recognize her . . . because her identity is fixed and indestructible, just as fixed and indestructible as the identity of God the Father and Jesus Christ the Son. . . . They cannot be changed; they are from everlasting to everlasting, eternally the same; so it will be with us. We will progress and develop and grow in wisdom and understanding, but our identity can never change" (*Gospel Doctrine,* 25). The doctrine of the eternal continuation of the soul and our individual identity is a grand message of peace, a comfort and consolation to mortals.

O death, where is thy sting? O grave, where is thy victory?
The sting of death is sin; and the strength of sin is the law.
But thanks be to God, which giveth us the victory
through our Lord Jesus Christ.
—I CORINTHIANS 15:55–57

The death of a righteous person, while sorrowful, has no devastating sting, for "those that die in me shall not taste of death, for it shall be sweet unto them" (D&C 42:46). The sweet assurance of continued life comes from the "firstfruits of them that slept" (I Corinthians 15:20). The prophet Abinadi taught: "And if Christ had not risen from the dead, or have broken the bands of death that the grave should have no victory, and that death should have no sting, there could have been no resurrection. But there is a resurrection, therefore the grave hath no victory, and the sting of death is swallowed up in Christ" (Mosiah 16:7–8). None of us is perfect in this life, but if we are firmly on the gospel path, our death can be sweet and our joy full.

Now he which stablisheth us with you in Christ,
and hath anointed us, is God; who hath also sealed us,
and given the earnest of the Spirit in our hearts.
—2 CORINTHIANS 1:21–22

What is our indication that we are on course, in line here for full salvation hereafter? "Hereby know we that we dwell in him, and he in us, because he hath given us of his Spirit" (1 John 4:13). The presence of God's Spirit is the divine assurance that we are headed in the right direction. It is God's seal, his attestation to us that he is serious about saving us. Indeed, the same Spirit that eventually seals us up unto eternal life places a seal of approval upon our lives here and now. Though the fulness of the blessings of eternal life are not available until the world to come, the peace and rest and hope that are harbingers of those unspeakable blessings can and should be ours in this world.

For we walk by faith, not by sight.
—2 CORINTHIANS 5:7

In 1833, the well-known English churchman John Henry Newman was homesick, seasick, and recovering from a bout with malaria. The ship was closed in by fog, the captain became disoriented, and all progress was halted for a week. In this dismal setting, Newman had little to do but wait, hope, and pray. Realizing his helplessness, he sought heaven's light. He found comfort as he wrote of his dependence on God:

> *Lead, kindly Light, amid th' encircling gloom,*
> *Lead thou me on!*
>
> . . . .
>
> *Keep thou my feet; I do not ask to see*
> *The distant scene—one step enough for me.*
> (Hymns, *no. 97*)

One faithful step to the edge of the light can bring more light. When we walk by faith through the fog and darkness of mortality, we can be directed, comforted, and saved by the Light of the World.

We pray you in Christ's stead, be ye reconciled to God.
For he [God the Father] hath made him [Christ]
to be sin for us, who knew no sin; that we might
be made the righteousness of God in him.
—2 CORINTHIANS 5:20–21

Jesus Christ came not only to change us but also to exchange with us. Paul explains in 2 Corinthians what someone has wisely called this "great exchange." Through the gospel covenant, Jesus offers to take our sin from us and put it upon himself. At the same time, he makes an offer that is almost unfathomable: he offers to impute to us his righteousness. We might be likened to a bucket of filthy water. When we enter into covenant with Christ, he takes the bucket and empties its foul contents. He then scours and scrubs the bucket until it shines brightly. When it is clean, the Master fills the newly cleansed container with living water. John said of him "that believeth" on the Lord Jesus, "out of his belly shall flow rivers of living water" (John 7:38).

For godly sorrow worketh repentance to salvation . . .
but the sorrow of the world worketh death.
—2 CORINTHIANS 7:10

Godly sorrow for sin is a sober recognition, not that we have been caught, nor that our deeds will prove embarrassing, but that we have sinned against God. Worldly sorrow results in frustration, anger, and bitterness. It leads to hardness of heart and stiff resistance to spiritual things. Godly sorrow leads us to true repentance and motivates us to confess and forsake our deeds, to commit to put such attitudes and actions out of our lives forever. It softens our hearts and makes us malleable and receptive to counsel and divine direction. In speaking to his errant son Corianton, Alma said: "And now, my son, I desire that ye should let these things trouble you no more, and only let your sins trouble you, with that trouble which shall bring you down unto repentance" (Alma 42:29). Godly sorrow entails seeing things as they really are—including ourselves, with all our sins and shortcomings—and then placing ourselves on the gospel path of recovery.

And he said unto me, My grace is sufficient for thee:
for my strength is made perfect in weakness.
Most gladly therefore will I rather glory in my infirmities,
that the power of Christ may rest upon me.
—2 CORINTHIANS 12:9

No one really knows what Paul's thorn in the flesh
was, but whatever it was, it kept Paul humble and
forced him to his knees. His inabilities and his impo-
tence in the face of this challenge were ever before
him. His thorn in the flesh occasioned seasons of
prayer, extended periods of wrestling and laboring in
the Spirit for a blessing that never came. Indeed, as he
suggests, another kind of blessing came—an acquaintance with Deity, a sanctified strength that came
through pain and suffering. When up against the wall
of faith, we can receive that enabling power we know
as the grace of Christ. As the Savior explained to
Moroni, when we acknowledge and confess our weakness—not only our specific weaknesses but our general mortal limitation—and submit ourselves to the
Lord, we allow him to transform weakness into
strength (Ether 12:27).

*I am crucified with Christ: nevertheless I live: yet not I,
but Christ liveth in me: and the life which I now live
in the flesh I live by the faith of the Son of God,
who loved me, and gave himself for me.*
—GALATIANS 2:20

Once we have committed our lives to Christ, we make our way down the strait and narrow path that eventually leads to life eternal. Such a trek is long and tiresome. Where do we find the strength we need? Do we simply work harder, double or triple our efforts, and hold on white-knuckled to the rod of iron until we fall down in exhaustion at the end of the path? Surely there is a better way! The Master calls us to surrender our burdens to him and find rest and peace (Matthew 11:28–30). Although, as Paul wrote, we have died as to the things of this world, in Christ we now live. God becomes our strength, empowering us through his Spirit. Thus our reliance is upon his mercy and grace, his enabling power to do what we could never do on our own.

*For as many of you as have been baptized into Christ have
put on Christ. There is neither Jew nor Greek, there
is neither bond nor free, there is neither male
nor female: for ye are all one in Christ Jesus.*
—GALATIANS 3:27–28

All who have come unto Christ and received his
gospel become members of the household of faith
and heirs to the blessings of the Father. There is no
aristocracy within the kingdom of God—no caste
system, no cliques based on money or chances for
learning—save only the aristocracy of faith and righteousness. We are a kingdom of brothers and sisters,
a church of equals. We are part of a divine system of
salvation in which plumbers preside over college presidents, homemakers instruct attorneys, and all dress
alike in the house of the Lord. Indeed, the Lord
"inviteth them all to come unto him and partake of his
goodness; and he denieth none that come unto him,
black and white, bond and free, male and female; and
he remembereth the heathen; and all are alike unto
God, both Jew and Gentile" (2 Nephi 26:33).

*But the fruit of the Spirit is love, joy, peace, longsuffering,
gentleness, goodness, faith, meekness, temperance. . . .
And they that are Christ's have crucified the flesh.*
—GALATIANS 5:22–25

Paul contrasts "works of the flesh"—such things as adultery, fornication, idolatry, hatred, and strife—with the fruit of the Spirit, those divine attributes that flow from a changed heart. Paul says essentially that if we claim membership in the Church of Jesus Christ, we ought to act accordingly. If we profess discipleship, people who observe us should be able to discern that discipleship. It's a wonderful thing to be a gospel scholar, but it's even more of a blessing to both know the doctrine and embody pure religion (James 1:27). It's a privilege to possess the gift of healing, to lay hands on the sick and, acting in behalf of the Lord, witness their recovery. It's a treasure beyond price to love others after the manner of our Master and witness the healing power of that love.

Whatsoever a man soweth, that shall he also reap. For he that soweth to his flesh shall of the flesh reap corruption; but he that soweth to the Spirit shall of the Spirit reap life everlasting.
—GALATIANS 6:7–8

The law of the harvest is that we reap what we sow. As a farmer harvests only what he has planted and nurtured, so will we receive spiritual blessings according to our faithfulness. In the kingdom of God there are no shortcuts. Just as you could not be a doctor without going to medical school, so you could not attain celestial glory if you had not prepared yourself to receive it. Likewise, it is not enough only to confess the name of Jesus; we must obey the laws and ordinances of the gospel. We are to keep the commandments and "press forward with a steadfastness in Christ, having a perfect brightness of hope, and a love of God and of all men" (2 Nephi 31:20). If with our hearts and actions we overcome the world and truly follow Jesus, we will avoid spiritual death and inherit eternal life.

That in the dispensation of the fulness of times he might gather together in one all things in Christ, both which are in heaven, and which are on earth; even in him.

—EPHESIANS 1:10

The phrase "the dispensation of the fulness of times" has special meaning to Latter-day Saints. We understand that the gospel is revealed from heaven in various time periods. "A dispensation of the gospel is a period of time in which the Lord has at least one authorized servant on the earth who bears the holy priesthood and the keys, and who has a divine commission to dispense the gospel to the inhabitants of the earth. When this occurs, the gospel is revealed anew, so that people of that dispensation do not have to depend basically on past dispensations for knowledge of the plan of salvation" (LDS Bible Dictionary, 657). The final dispensation, "the dispensation of the fulness of times" began in the spring of 1820 when darkness was dispersed, the heavens opened, and the Father and Son spoke to Joseph Smith. All of the streams of past dispensations flow into the ocean of the dispensation of the fulness of times.

For by grace are ye saved through faith; and that not of yourselves: it is the gift of God: not of works, lest any man should boast.
—EPHESIANS 2:8–9

Salvation is the greatest of all the gifts of God. It is not something that may be purchased, nor, in the strictest sense, is it something that may be earned. More correctly, salvation is a gift, something gloriously transcendent that may only be inherited and bestowed. Elder Bruce R. McConkie asked: "What salvation is free? What salvation comes by the grace of God? With all the emphasis of the rolling thunders of Sinai, we answer: All salvation is free; all comes by the merits and mercy and grace of the Holy Messiah; there is no salvation of any kind, nature, or degree that is not bound to Christ and his atonement" (*Promised Messiah,* 346–47). While our works of righteousness are necessary, they are not sufficient. God has done for us what we could never do for ourselves. That unmerited favor is what the scriptures call grace.

*Now therefore ye are no more strangers and foreigners,
but fellowcitizens with the saints, and of the household of God;
And are built upon the foundation of the apostles and prophets,
Jesus Christ himself being the chief corner stone.*
—EPHESIANS 2:19–20

Jesus described himself as the stone the builders had foolishly rejected but which had now become the chief cornerstone. Jacob prophesied that the Jews in Jesus' day would reject "the stone upon which they might build and have safe foundation" (Jacob 4:15). Christ is the cornerstone upon whom our salvation depends. Apostles are called to be special witnesses of the name of Christ in all the world and are set apart as legal administrators empowered to regulate the affairs of the Church wherever they go. As we gather into the gospel family, we become citizens in the kingdom of God on earth. We dwell together under the gospel roof, not as strangers but as fellowcitizens. With the apostles and prophets as the foundation and Christ as the chief cornerstone, we find refuge and salvation in the household of faith.

And he gave some, apostles; and some, prophets; and some,
evangelists; and some, pastors and teachers; for the
perfecting of the saints, for the work of the ministry,
for the edifying of the body of Christ.
—EPHESIANS 4:11–12

Paul explains that the organization of the Church is not only for efficiency in the labor of the ministry but also for the purpose of maintaining unity in doctrine and practice among the people of God. Like spiritual gifts, the offices and assignments within the Savior's Church work together to make the body of Christ perfect. Each person magnifying a calling contributes to the whole. The Church, a system of organized sacrifice, will thus be essential "till we all come in the unity of the faith, and of the knowledge of the Son of God, unto a perfect man . . . that we henceforth be no more children, tossed to and fro, and carried about with every wind of doctrine, . . . but speaking the truth in love, [we] may grow up into him in all things, which is the head, even Christ" (Ephesians 4:13–15).

*Wherefore take unto you the whole armour of God,
that ye may be able to withstand in the evil day,
and having done all, to stand.*
—Ephesians 6:13

Our mortal probation is a continuation of the war in heaven; it is a war with no neutral territory. We can gain the victory only by putting on the full armor of God. Our loins are girt about with enlightening truth. We put on the breastplate of righteousness to keep our heart tender and protected. Our feet are shod with the preparation of the gospel of peace that we might stay on the path of righteousness. We wear the helmet of the hope of salvation given to us by Christ. We hold up the shield of faith to safeguard truth. We wield the sword of the Spirit, or the word of God, to cut through worldly philosophies. We will stand with the righteous in the last days by putting on the whole armor of God.

*Being confident of this very thing, that he which hath
begun a good work in you will perform it
until the day of Jesus Christ.*
—PHILIPPIANS 1:6

One of the youngest sons in a large family had begun to wander from the strait path. Seeing the pain and frustration etched on his father's face one evening, and knowing very well that he was the cause of much of his parents' pain, he said, "Dad, please don't be too upset with me. The Lord's not finished with me yet." We simply cannot afford to give up on others—or ourselves. God is not finished with us yet. He who knows all things from beginning to end is working to bring each of us closer to him. As President Ezra Taft Benson said, "Men and women who turn their lives over to God will discover that He can make a lot more out of their lives than they can" (*Teachings of Ezra Taft Benson*, 361).

Let this mind be in you, which was also in Christ Jesus:
who, being in the form of God, thought it
not robbery to be equal with God.
—PHILIPPIANS 2:5–6

Like Christ, all men and women are made in the image and likeness of God, so it is neither robbery nor heresy for the children of God to aspire to be like God. Like any parent, our Heavenly Father wants his children to become all that he is. Godhood comes through overcoming the world through the Atonement, becoming heirs of God and joint-heirs with Christ, and thus inheriting all things, just as Jesus inherits all things. We will then be conformed to the image of the Lord Jesus, receive his glory, and be one with him and with the Father. In short, God is not of another species, nor is he the great unknowable one; he is indeed our Father in Heaven. He has revealed a plan whereby we might enjoy happiness in this world and both be like him and dwell with him in the world to come.

Wherefore, my beloved, as ye have always obeyed,
not as in my presence only, but now much more in my absence,
work out your own salvation with fear and trembling.
—PHILIPPIANS 2:12

The gospel of Jesus Christ is a gospel covenant, a two-way promise. God promises to do for us what we could never do for ourselves—forgive us, cleanse us, raise us from the dead, and qualify us for the highest heaven. At the same time, we agree to do what we can do—love God, exercise faith, repent, keep our covenants, and deny ourselves of all ungodliness. We must never suppose that we can actually work out our own salvation by doing it on our own. There simply are not enough charitable acts to do, meetings to attend, or prayers to utter to save ourselves. But we can stay on the gospel path and plead for his enabling power, "for it is God which worketh in you both to will and to do of his good pleasure" (Philippians 2:13).

I can do all things through Christ which strengtheneth me.
—PHILIPPIANS 4:13

With faith in the Lord Jesus Christ we can move mountains of difficulty and trouble. Vibrant faith in Jesus Christ makes and keeps us "strong and of a good courage" (Joshua 1:9). This faith comes from obedience to God's commandments and a sincere desire to do his will. Ammon said, "I know that I am nothing; as to my strength I am weak; therefore I will not boast of myself, but I will boast of my God, for in his strength I can do all things" (Alma 26:12). The Lord himself said, "I am the vine, ye are the branches: He that abideth in me, and I in him, the same bringeth forth much fruit: for without me ye can do nothing" (John 15:5). Only with Christ, who inspires, strengthens, and saves, can we do all things according to his will.

DECEMBER

For unto us a child is born,
unto us a son is given: and the government
shall be upon his shoulder: and his name
shall be called Wonderful, Counsellor, The
mighty God, The everlasting Father,
The Prince of Peace.

—ISAIAH 9:6

Despise not prophesyings. Prove all things;
hold fast that which is good.

—1 THESSALONIANS 5:20–21

The gift of prophecy is abundantly found in the Lord's Church. As members of his Church, we are to embrace the spirit of prophecy: "Deny not the spirit of revelation, nor the spirit of prophecy, for wo unto him that denieth these things" (D&C 11:25). Likewise, revelation is the bedrock foundation of the restored gospel. By revelation we know that Jesus is the Christ (Revelation 19:10). By revelation we know the truth of all things (Moroni 10:4–5), and we are able to discern light and darkness and gain wisdom (1 John 4:1–6; D&C 50:23–25). In the spirit of revelation, we are to examine, or put to the test, all things; we are to study and humbly approach the Lord in prayer to find answers to our questions (D&C 9:7–9).

For this is good and acceptable in the sight of God our Saviour;
who is willing to have all men to be saved, and to come unto the
knowledge of the truth which is in Christ Jesus.
—JST 1 TIMOTHY 2:3–4

There is no ceiling on the number of saved beings;
God desires to save all of his children. "We believe that
through the Atonement of Christ, all mankind may be
saved, by obedience to the laws and ordinances of the
Gospel" (Articles of Faith 1:3). Thus we take the message of salvation to every nation, kindred, tongue, and
people, in fulfillment of the Lord's commission to
preach the gospel to every creature (Matthew 28:19;
Mark 16:15–16; D&C 68:8–9). Likewise, we perform
vicarious ordinances in the temple for individuals who
did not have the opportunity to receive those ordinances in this life. "The Lord is not slack concerning
his promise and coming, . . . but long-suffering toward
us, not willing that any should perish, but that all
should come to repentance" (JST 2 Peter 3:9).

For there is one God, and one mediator between
God and men, the man Christ Jesus.
—1 TIMOTHY 2:5

Each of us falls short, and Jesus is our only hope. Elder Boyd K. Packer taught: "Each of us lives on a kind of spiritual credit. One day the account will be closed, a settlement demanded. However casually we may view it now, when that day comes and the fore-closure is imminent, we will look around in restless agony for someone, anyone, to help us. And, by eternal law, mercy cannot be extended save there be one who is both willing and able to assume our debt and pay the price and arrange the terms for our redemption. Unless there is a mediator, unless we have a friend, the full weight of justice untempered, unsympathetic, must, positively must fall on us. . . . But know this: Truth, glorious truth, proclaims there is such a Mediator. . . . Through Him mercy can be fully extended to each of us without offending the eternal law of justice" (Conference Report, April 1977, 80). Our Lord offers to reclaim us, redeem us, restore us.

Be thou an example of the believers, in word, in conversation,
in charity, in spirit, in faith, in purity.
—1 TIMOTHY 4:12

The example of our Christian living will convey a far greater message than will all the preaching in the world. To lift others and inspire them in the direction of gospel light, we must stand on higher ground. No holier-than-thou attitude, no smugness or self-righteousness can be found in those who sincerely seek to emulate Jesus. True followers of the Master strive daily to do as he would do. "As His followers, we cannot do a mean or shoddy or ungracious thing without tarnishing His image," taught President Gordon B. Hinckley. "Nor can we do a good and gracious and generous act without burnishing more brightly the symbol of Him whose name we have taken upon ourselves. Our lives must become a symbol of meaningful expression, the symbol of our declaration of our testimony of the living Christ, the Eternal Son of the living God" (*Teachings of Gordon B. Hinckley*, 184).

*For the grace of God which bringeth salvation to all men,
hath appeared; teaching us that, denying ungodliness
and worldly lusts, we should live soberly,
righteously, and godly, in this present world.*
—JST Titus 2:11–12

While the fulness of salvation is freely available to every son and daughter of God, only those who become "disciples indeed" (John 8:31) qualify for the association of holy beings hereafter. That discipleship, linked inextricably with happiness in this world and in the world to come, entails a godly walk and conversation, a serious effort to deny ourselves of ungodliness and worldly lusts and separate ourselves from sin, which deadens and desensitizes the soul. We are able to put off the world only by putting on Christ. Thus Alma taught Helaman that he should "withstand every temptation of the devil" through his "faith on the Lord Jesus Christ" (Alma 37:33).

*For we have not an high priest which cannot be touched with
the feeling of our infirmities; but was in all points
tempted like as we are, yet without sin.*
—HEBREWS 4:15

In thought, word, and deed, Jesus alone is the Sinless One. He fully kept all gospel laws. His love was perfect; his life sublime. But he was not without temptation, sorrow and suffering, or hunger and thirst. Jesus overcame the world, learning by experience the heartache that pervades so much of our lives. He took upon himself the infirmities of all of us so that his bowels "may be filled with mercy, according to the flesh, that he may know according to the flesh how to succor his people according to their infirmities" (Alma 7:12). We cannot tell him anything about anguish. We cannot complain that he doesn't understand our misery. He knows, he understands, he stands ready and willing to give rest to our souls. This is the unfathomable love, mercy, and grace of our Savior.

Now faith is the substance of things hoped for,
the evidence of things not seen.
—HEBREWS 11:1

All prophets exhort and exemplify faith as a vital principle of the gospel. Joseph Smith taught that faith is not just a principle of the gospel but "the first principle in revealed religion, and the foundation of all righteousness" (*Lectures on Faith,* 1:1). It is by faith that the brother of Jared moved mount Zerin, "and if he had not had faith it would not have moved; wherefore *thou workest after men have faith*" (Ether 12:30; italics added). We have been told to "remember that without faith you can do nothing; therefore ask in faith" (D&C 8:10). Faith in the Lord is both a principle of action that leads to repentance and a power that leads to good works. Faith is essential to salvation and is a gift of God to those who seek it.

But without faith it is impossible to please [God]:
for he that cometh to God must believe that he is,
and that he is a rewarder of them that diligently seek him.
—HEBREWS 11:6

God desires all of his children to come to him. But we cannot do so without faith. The Prophet Joseph Smith said: "If it should be asked—Why is it impossible to please God without faith? The answer would be—Because without faith it is impossible for men to be saved; and as God desires the salvation of men, he must, of course, desire that they should have faith; and he could not be pleased unless they had, or else he could be pleased with their destruction. . . . When men begin to live by faith they begin to draw near to God; and when faith is perfected they are like him; and because he is saved they are saved also; for they will be in the same situation he is in, because they have come to him; and when he appears they shall be like him, for they will see him as he is" (*Lectures on Faith,* 7:7–8).

And these all [the ancient Saints], having obtained a good report
through faith, received not the promise: God having
provided some better thing for us, that they
without us should not be made perfect.
—HEBREWS 11:39–40

Salvation is a family affair. Elijah came to the
Kirtland Temple in April 1836 to "turn the heart of
the fathers to the children, and the heart of the children to their fathers, lest [the Lord] come and smite
the earth with a curse" (Malachi 4:6). It was revealed
through Joseph Smith that "the earth will be smitten
with a curse unless there is a welding link of some kind
or other between the fathers and the children. . . . For
we without them cannot be made perfect; neither can
they without us be made perfect" (D&C 128:18). The
Prophet further taught that "it is necessary that the
sealing power should be in our hands to seal our children and our dead for the fullness of the dispensation
of times" (*Teachings of the Prophet Joseph Smith,* 356). The
holy temple becomes the eternal link between past
and present, between the living and the dead.

If any of you lack wisdom, let him ask of God,
that giveth to all men liberally, and upbraideth not;
and it shall be given him.
—JAMES 1:5

The young Joseph Smith acted in faith upon the words of James. "This single verse of scripture has had a greater impact and a more far reaching effect upon mankind that any other single sentence ever recorded by any prophet in any age," Elder Bruce R. McConkie wrote. "It might well be said that the crowning act of the ministry of James was not his martyrdom for the testimony of Jesus, but his recitation, as guided by the Holy Ghost, of these simple words which led to the opening of the heavens in modern times. And it might well be added that every investigator of revealed truth stands, at some time in the course of his search, in the place where Joseph Smith stood" (*Doctrinal New Testament Commentary*, 3:246–47). The Lord does not upbraid or find fault with our feeble but honest inquiries; rather, he rewards us liberally for coming unto him.

But be ye doers of the word, and not hearers only,
deceiving your own selves.
—JAMES 1:22

The Saints are to be the light of the world, a city set on a hill so that others see our good works and glorify God. Although it is supremely important that we know the word of God, we must do more. We are to live the gospel, not just listen to it. Wholly relying upon the grace of God, we must be "anxiously engaged in a good cause, and do many things of [our] own free will, and bring to pass much righteousness" (D&C 58:27). Our faith is shown in our commitment to strive to put into practice the teachings of the Master. We are to become such a positive force for good that the world will be constrained to acknowledge the power of God in us (D&C 105:32). This can come only as we do what we have heard.

Pure religion and undefiled before God and the Father is this,
To visit the fatherless and widows in their affliction,
and to keep himself unspotted from the world.
—JAMES 1:27

Religion is a matter of the heart, of devotion and conviction; a matter of the soul, of personal conversion; and a matter of service and sacrifice, of being willing to be inconvenienced and to lift and lighten the burdens of others. Jesus not only knew certain truths but embodied truth. Jesus *was* truth. No one understood the doctrine of consecration better than the Lord himself. It wasn't the Master's knowledge of consecration that made him who he was, however; rather, he was who he was because he was fully and completely consecrated. The Prophet Joseph Smith taught that "to be justified before God we must love one another: we must overcome evil; we must visit the fatherless and the widow in their affliction, and we must keep ourselves unspotted from the world: for such virtues flow from the great fountain of pure religion" (*Teachings of the Prophet Joseph Smith*, 76).

*Thou believest that there is one God; thou doest well: the devils
also believe, and tremble. But wilt thou know,
O vain man, that faith without works is dead?*
—JAMES 2:19—20

Satan knows that Jesus is the Christ; he knows the scriptures and can surely quote holy writ. But he is the devil because of what he does. It is in what we do—our actions as well as our thoughts and desires—that we become either like Satan or like Christ. As we choose to follow the Savior, we become more like him. It is by our works that our faith in the Lord is manifest, made perfect and real. Just as the body without the spirit is dead, so there is no life in faith that does not include works (James 2:26). A person with strong faith is a person who acts upon belief. Those who possess active faith do the works of righteousness—humbly serving and obeying. Our good works are faith and love in action.

*Confess your faults one to another, and pray one for another,
that ye may be healed. The effectual fervent prayer
of a righteous man availeth much.*
—JAMES 5:16

Prayer and confession are to be performed meekly
and with full purpose of heart. With godly sorrow, we
confess our sins, and with humility we open our souls
to heaven and pray for help, comfort, and peace. Who
among us has not offered heartfelt prayers to God for
blessing and protection? Prayer is a constant part of
the disciple's life. President Harold B. Lee taught:
"The prized knowledge that we can possess is that the
Lord hears and answers prayers. . . . Praying is not just
a matter of saying words, . . . but [recognizing] that
God, our Heavenly Father, and His Son, Jesus Christ,
are living, real personalities and that through the ministry of the other member of the Godhead, the Holy
Ghost, . . . we can . . . receive an answer to our inquiry
and strength for our days" (*Harold B. Lee,* 53).

Brethren, if any of you do err from the truth, and one convert
him; let him know, that he which converteth the sinner
from the error of his way shall save a soul from death,
and shall hide a multitude of sins.

—JAMES 5:19–20

King Benjamin spoke of obtaining a remission of
sins through putting off the natural man and putting
on Christ (Mosiah 3:17–19). He also explained how
we may keep a remission of sins: "For the sake of
retaining a remission of your sins from day to day, that
ye may walk guiltless before God—I would that ye
should impart of your substance to the poor, . . . both
spiritually and temporally, according to their wants"
(Mosiah 4:26). We enjoy the blessings of the Master
in our personal lives to the extent that we are engaged
in the work of the Master—in blessing others. The
early elders of this dispensation were thus instructed
to "thrust in your sickle with all your soul, and your
sins are forgiven you" (D&C 31:5). In short, we save
more than one person when we lead another soul to
salvation.

*But as he which hath called you is holy, so be ye holy in
all manner of conversation; because it is written,
Be ye holy; for I am holy.*
—1 PETER 1:15–16

In all ages of time, whenever the gospel of Jesus
Christ has been on earth, God has commissioned his
children to "be a special people unto himself, above
all people that are upon the face of the earth"
(Deuteronomy 7:6). It has always been necessary for
those who aspired to holiness to "put [a] difference
between holy and unholy, and between unclean and
clean" (Leviticus 10:10), to draw the line between
righteousness and unrighteousness. The Prophet
Joseph declared, "When I contemplate the rapidity
with which the great and glorious day of the coming
of the Son of Man advances, . . . I cry out in my heart,
What manner of persons ought we to be in all holy
conversation and godliness!" (*Teachings of the Prophet
Joseph Smith,* 29). The Saints of the Most High are
called to be holy, to separate themselves from the
world while remaining in the world.

Ye are a chosen generation, a royal priesthood, an holy
nation, a peculiar people; that ye should shew forth
the praises of him who hath called you out of
darkness into his marvellous light.
—1 PETER 2:9

The Saints of God are called to be a chosen generation, a peculiar people. In addition to acknowledging
that we are a purchased people and thus that we are
not our own, we are also called upon to stand apart
from the world and from worldliness. We are peculiar
in that we are different—our standards, our taste, and
our style of life. Because we have left the darkness of
the world and come into the marvelous light of the
gospel of Jesus Christ, we cannot afford to compromise our commitment or dilute our discipleship. Our
heart is in Zion, our place with the people of God.

*But sanctify the Lord God in your hearts: and be ready always
to give an answer to every man that asketh you a reason
of the hope that is in you with meekness and fear.*
—1 PETER 3:15

None of us knows all of the answers to all of the questions. For that matter, the Lord has not chosen to reveal everything yet. And so it is commendable to confess our ignorance and at the same time profess our witness of the truth of the gospel. On the other hand, the Lord and his Church desperately need competent and capable witnesses, men and women of faith whose conviction is as satisfying to the mind as it is soothing and settling to the heart. The Lord needs people in his kingdom who have obtained a reason for the hope within them. While we can never in this life know everything, we can know some things, and we need to be in a position to defend the faith as effectively as both human reason and divine revelation allow.

For this cause was the gospel preached also to them that are dead,
that they might be judged according to men in the flesh,
but live according to God in the spirit.
—1 PETER 4:6

While Jesus' body lay in the tomb, the living Christ went to further the Father's work by offering salvation to the dead. He ministered to the righteous in the spirit world. As prophesied by Isaiah, he went "to open the blind eyes, to bring out the prisoners from the prison, and them that sit in darkness out of the prison house" (Isaiah 42:7). Missionary work among the dead was commenced by Christ and continues today by his authorized messengers in the spirit world. Christ's atonement was offered not just for those few who lived on the earth in the meridian of time, nor for those billions who have lived since and before, but for all inhabitants of the earth—past, present, and future. The loving mercy and perfect justice of God's plan are manifest fully in the doctrine of salvation for the dead.

Give diligence to make your calling and election sure:
for if ye do these things, ye shall never fall: For so an entrance
shall be ministered unto you abundantly into the everlasting
kingdom of our Lord and Saviour Jesus Christ.
—2 PETER 1:10–11

Those who conduct themselves with fidelity and devotion to God and his laws shall eventually know the peace that "passeth all understanding" (Philippians 4:7), the calming, powerful assurance that one has successfully met the challenges of mortality. These are they who have lived by every word of God and are willing to serve the Lord at all hazards. Though it is true that the fulness of eternal life is not attainable in this life, such peace is attainable here and now. "But blessed are they who are faithful and endure, whether in life or in death, for they shall inherit eternal life" (D&C 50:5). We have the scriptural promise that faithfully enduring to the end leads to the promise of eternal life, whether that promise be received here or hereafter.

If we say that we have no sin, we deceive ourselves,
and the truth is not in us.
—1 JOHN 1:8

The psalmist wrote: "There is none that doeth good, no, not one" (Psalm 14:3). Likewise, the apostle Paul declared, "All have sinned, and come short of the glory of God" (Romans 3:23). No person who comes into this life, save Jesus only, lives without sin. Not the mightiest apostle or the greatest prophet is able to navigate a perfect course through mortality. Thus, none of us can be bold enough to demand association with holy beings in the life to come as a result of our "earned" perfection. In our present condition, unaided, we cannot make it. But that knowledge moves us to confess our weakness and turn to him who did live the law of God perfectly, even the Lord Jesus Christ.

Whosoever is born of God doth not commit sin;
for his seed remaineth in him: and he cannot commit sin,
because he is born of God.
—1 JOHN 3:9

Many of us know people who clearly enjoy the blessings of the gospel and who have been born of the Spirit. But even they make mistakes. The Prophet Joseph Smith altered 1 John 3:9 in his inspired translation of the Bible. "Whosoever is born of God," the corrected passage reads, "doth not continue in sin." Those who have walked in the light of the Lord and who step temporarily into the darkness want to escape from the darkness and return, as quickly as possible, to the light. They cannot continue in sin, for their consciences, now refined by the power of the Holy Ghost, will not allow them to do so. Truly, "if we walk in the light, as [Christ] is in the light, we have fellowship one with another, and the blood of Jesus Christ his Son cleanseth us from all sin" (1 John 1:7).

Beloved, let us love one another: for love is of God; and every one that loveth is born of God, and knoweth God. He that loveth not knoweth not God; for God is love.

—1 JOHN 4:7–8

Love is the very essence of the gospel of Jesus Christ and a sure indication of our Christian conversion. It is a verb that moves us to action and inspires kindness and compassion. Love is a solemn responsibility to act in behalf of each other, our spouse and children, and future generations. It is multidimensional, involving heart, might, mind, and soul. Love has transforming power that helps individuals and families realize their divine nature as daughters and sons of God. True love is its own reward; the more you give, the more you will receive. It grows as we serve and sacrifice for one another. Ultimately, love is a gift from God (Moroni 7:47–48).

There is no fear in love; but perfect love casteth out fear:
because fear hath torment. He that feareth
is not made perfect in love.
—1 JOHN 4:18

The love of God settles human hearts. President Thomas S. Monson taught: "Our opportunities to give of ourselves are indeed limitless, but they are also perishable. . . . My brothers and sisters, may we resolve from this day forward to fill our hearts with love. May we go the extra mile to include in our lives any who are lonely or downhearted or who are suffering in any way. May we '[cheer] up the sad and [make] someone feel glad' (*Hymns,* no. 223). May we live so that when that final summons is heard, we may have no serious regrets, no unfinished business, but will be able to say with the Apostle Paul, 'I have fought a good fight, I have finished my course, I have kept the faith' (2 Tim. 4:7)" (Conference Report, October 2001, 72, 74).

Whosoever believeth that Jesus is the Christ is born of God.
—1 JOHN 5:1

A fundamental manifestation of a new birth in Christ is the conviction that Jesus is the Son of God and that he has done for us what no one else could do. President Howard W. Hunter said: "It is possible for Christ to be born in men's lives, and when such an experience actually happens, a man is 'in Christ'— Christ is 'formed' in him. This presupposes that we take Christ into our hearts and make him the living contemporary of our lives. He is not just a general truth or a fact in history but also the Savior of men everywhere and at all times. . . . The real Christmas comes to him who has taken Christ into his life as a moving, dynamic, vitalizing force. The real spirit of Christmas lies in the life and mission of the Master" (*Real Christmas,* 4–5). In the truest sense, then, we celebrate Christmas when we celebrate the birth of Christ not only in the world but in our individual hearts.

*I have no greater joy than to hear that
my children walk in the truth.*
—3 JOHN 1:4

President Gordon B. Hinckley has said: "What a glorious and beautiful thing it is to see the child of your dreams walk with head up, standing tall, unafraid, and with confidence, taking advantage of the tremendous opportunities that open around him or her. Isaiah said, 'All thy children shall be taught of the Lord; and great shall be the peace of thy children' (Isa. 54:13). So lead your sons and daughters, so guide and direct them from the time they are very small, so teach them in the ways of the Lord, that peace will be their companion throughout life" (*Ensign,* November 2000, 97–100). The family is the most important unit in time and in eternity. Truly, the deepest joys are family joys.

Behold, I stand at the door, and knock: if any man hear
my voice, and open the door, I will come in to him,
and will sup with him, and he with me.
—REVELATION 3:20

The Lord desires that we develop the attributes of godliness so that we can experience a fulness of joy and be endowed with his glory. He stands ready to forgive, tutor, and exalt. "Draw near unto me and I will draw near unto you; seek me diligently and ye shall find me; ask, and ye shall receive; knock, and it shall be opened unto you" (D&C 88:63). If we truly humble ourselves, repent, and overcome worldly susceptibilities, we will be given a crown of righteousness, glory, honor, immortality, and eternal life. As "heirs of God, and joint-heirs with Christ" (Romans 8:17), we will rule and reign on heavenly thrones forever, inherit all that the Father hath, and be "made partakers of the glories" (D&C 133:57). This is our calling, our potential, and the great promise of the plan of salvation.

And they overcame [Lucifer] by the blood of the Lamb,
and by the word of their testimony;
and they loved not their lives unto the death.
—REVELATION 12:11

The modern day is a singular time, an unusual era that requires singular and unusual souls to bring order out of spreading chaos. That's the daunting task before us, but surely we are up to it. We need not fret or fear, for "they that be with us are more than they that be with them" (2 Kings 6:16). We are here not by chance but rather by design, as part of a grand plan of salvation. We are not novices in championing eternal causes or confronting organized evil. We are seasoned veterans, for we already have the experience of standing valiantly on the side of Elohim, Jehovah, and Michael and opposing the forces of Lucifer in a distant past. We defeated him once, and we will do it again, "by the blood of the Lamb, and by the word of [our] testimony" (Revelation 12:11).

And I saw another angel fly in the midst of heaven, having the everlasting gospel to preach unto them that dwell on the earth, and to every nation, and kindred, and tongue, and people.
—REVELATION 14:6

John's vision of the angel in the midst of heaven foretells the latter-day restoration of the gospel. Not only would one angel, Moroni, restore the word of God through the coming forth of the Book of Mormon, but other angels would restore power and authority to God's kingdom on earth. The Prophet Joseph Smith told of "divers angels, . . . all declaring their dispensation, their rights, their keys, their honors, their majesty and glory, and the power of their priesthood; giving line upon line, precept upon precept; here a little, and there a little" (D&C 128:21). Truly, the heavens were opened, and the everlasting gospel was revealed anew. Just as angels announced "good tidings of great joy" (Luke 2:10) at the birth of our Savior, so God again spoke to man through holy angels and ushered in the dispensation of the fulness of times.

And God shall wipe away all tears from their eyes; and there shall
be no more death, neither sorrow, nor crying, neither shall there
be any more pain: for the former things are passed away.
—REVELATION 21:4

The great millennial day commences the judgment
of the inhabitants of the earth, both past and present.
Satan will be bound and the wicked destroyed. Christ
will reign personally upon the earth, and all things will
be renewed and revealed. Death, sorrow, and disease
will cease. "And there shall be no sorrow because there
is no death. In that day an infant shall not die until he
is old; and his life shall be as the age of a tree; and
when he dies he shall not sleep, that is to say in the
earth, but shall be changed in the twinkling of an eye,
and shall be caught up, and his rest shall be glorious"
(D&C 101:29–31). What a magnificent time of peace
and rest for those Saints who have overcome the world
and become sons and daughters of God.

He which testifieth these things saith,
Surely I come quickly. Amen. Even so, come, Lord Jesus.
—REVELATION 22:20

In time's meridian, Jesus was born in Bethlehem. Fulfilling prophecy, he brought purpose to the confused, healing to the wounded, knowledge to the ignorant, and hope to the disconsolate. He died at the hands of wicked men, rose from the grave, and ascended into heaven. That same Jesus appeared with his Father to a fourteen-year old boy in upstate New York in the spring of 1820. Their grand work of restoration will continue to spread until the knowledge of a Savior is brought to every nation, kindred, tongue, and people. And then the Lord Jesus will return. "Wherefore, may the kingdom of God go forth, that the kingdom of heaven may come, that thou, O God, mayest be glorified in heaven so on earth, that thine enemies may be subdued; for thine is the honor, power and glory, forever and ever. Amen" (D&C 65:6).

SOURCES

Benson, Ezra Taft. *Come unto Christ*. Salt Lake City: Deseret Book, 1983.

——. *The Teachings of Ezra Taft Benson*. Salt Lake City: Bookcraft, 1988.

——. *A Witness and a Warning*. Salt Lake City: Deseret Book, 1988.

Dew, Sheri L. *Go Forward with Faith: The Biography of Gordon B. Hinckley*. Salt Lake City: Deseret Book, 1996.

Hafen, Bruce C., and Marie K. Hafen. *The Belonging Heart: The Atonement and Relationships with God and Family*. Salt Lake City: Deseret Book, 1994.

Harold B. Lee. Vol. [2] of Teachings of Presidents of the Church series. Salt Lake City: The Church of Jesus Christ of Latter-day Saints, 2000.

Hinckley, Gordon B. *Teachings of Gordon B. Hinckley*. Salt Lake City: Deseret Book, 1997.

Hunter, Howard W. *The Real Christmas*. Salt Lake City: Bookcraft, 1994.

Hymns of The Church of Jesus Christ of Latter-day Saints. Salt Lake

City: The Church of Jesus Christ of Latter-day Saints, 1985.

Joseph F. Smith. Vol. [1] of *Teachings of Presidents of the Church* series. Salt Lake City: The Church of Jesus Christ of Latter-day Saints, 1998.

Journal of Discourses. 26 vols. London: Latter-day Saints' Book Depot, 1854–86.

Kimball, Spencer W. *The Teachings of Spencer W. Kimball*. Edited by Edward L. Kimball. Salt Lake City: Bookcraft, 1982.

Lee, Harold B. *Stand Ye in Holy Places: Selected Sermons and Writings of President Harold B. Lee*. Salt Lake City: Deseret Book, 1974.

Lewis, C. S. *Mere Christianity*. New York: Macmillan, 1981.

Lowell, James Russell. *The Vision of Sir Launfal*. Boston: Ticknor and Fields, 1867.

MacArthur, John F., Jr. *Faith Works: The Gospel According to Jesus*. Rev. ed. Grand Rapids, Mich.: Zondervan, 1994.

McConkie, Bruce R. *Doctrinal New Testament Commentary*. 3 vols. Salt Lake City: Bookcraft, 1965–73.

———. *The Mortal Messiah*. 4 vols. Salt Lake City: Deseret Book, 1979–81.

———. *A New Witness for the Articles of Faith*. Salt Lake City: Deseret Book, 1985.

———. *The Promised Messiah*. Salt Lake City: Deseret Book, 1978.

McKay, David O. *Gospel Ideals.* Salt Lake City: Improvement Era, 1953.

———. *Man May Know for Himself.* Compiled by Claire Middlemiss. Salt Lake City: Deseret Book, 1967.

———. *True to the Faith: Sermons and Writings of David O. McKay.* Comp. Llewelyn R. McKay. Salt Lake City: Bookcraft, 1966.

Morris, Leon. *The Gospel According to Matthew.* Grand Rapids, Mich.: Eerdmans, 1992.

Packer, Boyd K. *Let Not Your Heart Be Troubled.* Salt Lake City: Bookcraft, 1991.

Selections from Doctrines of Salvation. Salt Lake City: The Church of Jesus Christ of Latter-day Saints, 2001.

Smith, Joseph. *Lectures on Faith.* Compiled by N. B. Lundwall. Salt Lake City: Deseret Book, 1985.

———. *Teachings of the Prophet Joseph Smith.* Selected by Joseph Fielding Smith. Salt Lake City: Deseret Book, 1976.

Smith, Joseph F. *Gospel Doctrine.* Salt Lake City: Deseret Book, 1998.

Smith, Joseph Fielding. *Doctrines of Salvation.* Compiled by Bruce R. McConkie. 3 vols. Salt Lake City: Bookcraft, 1954–56.

Stanley, Charles. *The Wonderful, Spirit-Filled Life.* Nashville, Tenn.: Thomas Nelson Publishers, 1992.

Talmage, James E. *Jesus the Christ.* Salt Lake City: Deseret Book, 1915.

About the Authors

Robert L. Millet and Lloyd D. Newell are both members of the Religious Education faculty at Brigham Young University.

Brother Millet, professor of ancient scripture and former dean of Religious Education, is the author of numerous books, including *I Will Fear No Evil, More Holiness Give Me,* and *Alive in Christ.* He and his wife, Shauna, are the parents of six children.

Brother Newell has been the announcer for the Mormon Tabernacle Choir broadcast of "Music and the Spoken Word" for more than a decade. He also serves as an associate faculty member of the School of Family Life at BYU and is the author of two books, *The Divine Connection* and *May Peace Be with You.* Lloyd and his wife, Karmel, are the parents of four children.